Ecosystems Knowledge

Digital Tools and Uses Set

coordinated by
Imad Saleh

Volume 6

Ecosystems Knowledge

*Modeling and Analysis Method for
Information and Communication*

Samuel Szoniecky

WILEY

First published 2018 in Great Britain and the United States by ISTE Ltd and John Wiley & Sons, Inc.

ISTE Ltd
27-37 St George's Road
London SW19 4EU
UK

www.iste.co.uk

John Wiley & Sons, Inc.
111 River Street
Hoboken, NJ 07030
USA

www.wiley.com

Library of Congress Control Number: 2018935807

British Library Cataloguing-in-Publication Data
A CIP record for this book is available from the British Library
ISBN 978-1-78630-064-5

Contents

Introduction

> The multiple modes of recognition
> and knowledge, by analogy,
> are inherent to any cognitive activity
> and to all thought.
> *Edgard Morin*

> It would be quite illusory to think
> that we could do without
> metaphor in order to qualify
> new objects.
> *Yves Jeanneret*

This book presents the concept of the knowledge ecosystem from the point of view of the uses, theory and design of a platform for collective intelligence. The aim is to provide conceptual and computational tools with which we can analyze the complexity of information and communication through a generic modeling of info-communication existences.

The concept of the ecosystem is increasingly used to describe situations in which multiple actors have dynamic relationships. These include the ecosystems of digital economy or those of innovation. The *Société française des sciences de l'information et de la communication* or SFIC (the French Society of Information and Communication Sciences) is positioning itself within the field of digital humanities through the discourse of a "complex ecosystem"[1]. However, to date, there has been no book that presents this

---

1 The web links for this book were verified on June 26, 2017.
http://www.sfsic.org/index.php/infos/lettres-sic-infos/archive/view/listid-1/mailid-336-flash-infos-manifeste-sic-et-ds-dh

concept in a detailed and critical way. Similarly, there is no book which deals with the use of this concept within a generic method of analysis of info-communication processes.

Nevertheless, the issue is important; it affects all individuals concerned with a "knowledge society" [LYO 79, COL 15], and especially with the intellectual technologies that can manage it [SAD 15, VIE 15]. In this context, where digital data is becoming increasingly important, it is fundamental to understand and manage the ins and outs of these technologies, the information they produce and the communications that they generate. This is one of the main themes advocated in France by the *Conseil national du numérique* or CNN (National Digital Council) in its 2015 report on digital ambition:

"For individuals, this right to self-determination implies that they have access to this data, that they can read, modify, erase and choose what they want to do with it; but moreover, also decide which services have access to it" [CNN 15, p. 50].

Faced with these challenges and with the goal of helping people understand these issues, Joi Ito, the director of MIT Media Lab, offers principles to "live by":

– "disobedience over compliance;

– pull over push;

– compasses over maps;

– learning over education;

– resilience over strength;

– risk over safety;

– practice over theory;

– diversity over ability;

– systems over objects;

– emergence over authority" [ITO 16][2].

---

2 We are using the translation proposed here: http://www.internetactu.net/2017/02/15/vers-lintelligence-etendue

Even if we cannot eliminate a form of provocation that is inherent to these propositions, we nevertheless wonder about the scope of such a discourse, for instance, when it is presented to a class of primary school children and their capacity to understand these principles, and especially to put them into practice. However, this is exactly our primary ambition: how can we make the mastery of knowledge accessible to as many people as possible? Can we accompany individuals in their discoveries of the world and provide them with the tools that will help them to perfect their learning? Can we design intellectual technologies to collectively increase the power of each person to take action?

To the questions of accompanying humans in their understanding of contemporary worlds through digital technologies, the control of non-biological existences which populate our ecosystems, in particular within the framework of the Internet of Things are added [SAL 17]. As the European Parliament concerns about civil law issues with regard to robotics show and the importance of designing a European agency to deal with these issues, it is important to know about these digital existences that are increasingly autonomous and ubiquitous [NOY 17]. Faced with this proliferation of "living" things, we need generic methods that help us understand what these digital existences are in order to control the consequences of their use, especially when these things are used in knowledge processes that trace the least learning activity. How can we evaluate the power of a digital object to take action r within an ecosystem? How can we control the information that these digital existences draw from our use of them?

The management of knowledge ecosystems by modeling the digital existences that populate them is also an important issue in digital humanities and more generally in the use of intellectual technologies [SZO 17a]. In this field, the multiplication of data and the algorithms that manipulate them sometimes obscures the reasoning and interpretations supported by the researchers. Can generic modeling be used to quantify and qualify the knowledge convened in the scientific discourse? Do these models provide an effective way to compare these discourses and use these comparisons to make recommendations?

In this work, we propose an analytical method of information and communication that uses the analogy of the ecosystem to embrace all the complexity of this field. After a presentation on the uses of the concept of ecosystem and its derivatives (nature, ecology, environment, etc.) on the

Web (Chapter 1: Use of the Ecosystem Concept on the Web), we will detail our method of analysis. This method is based on the generic modeling of info-communication existences (Chapter 2: Ecosystem Modeling: A Generic Method of Analysis), which uses theoretical principles (Chapter 3: Fundamental Principles for Modeling an Existence) and graphs (Chapter 4: Graphical Specifications for Modeling Existences). Based on these principles, we present the technological frameworks that we use to develop a collective intelligence platform dedicated to knowledge management (Chapter 5: Web Platform Specifications for Knowledge Ecosystems). Finally, we will present the research tracks and experiments that still need to be carried out in order to further explore the field of knowledge ecosystems (Conclusion).

1

Use of the Ecosystem Concept on the Web

> The animal and the environment
> are two sides of the same process,
> the object and the subject of knowledge
> mutually defining one another.
> *Humberto Maturana*

> Without a doubt, ecology drives you mad;
> that is where one should start.
> *Bruno Latour*

The concept of the ecosystem only appeared comparatively recently and has since been credited to the British ecologist Tansley, who first used the word in 1935. According to Dury, Tansley defines this concept as "a whole constructed by the relations that maintains the living species and the physical habitat that allows them to develop". Moreover, he highlights the shifting nature of this arrangement: "It depends on exogenous or external factors such as temperature, sunlight, humidity, etc., and internal factors such as the population sizes of the living beings that occupy it. The ecosystem is constantly changing according to these factors" [DUR 99, p. 488].

However, long before this word appeared in the field of ecology, we find intellectual practices that hypothesize a system of relations between living populations. Above all, some of these make the link between the organization of living beings and that of knowledge. We think, for example, of the notion of a garden which throughout antiquity up until today has been used as an analogy to reflect upon the human condition in relation to knowledge [HAR 07], or alternatively, to the I Ching, a complex theory that transposed the vicissitude of natural elements so as to model archetypes based on human behavior and the contrivance of these transformations, just as the alchemists of the European Middle Ages did [JUN 88], preoccupations that continue to be prominent in the writings of Haeckel, one of the inventors of ecology that bases this new science on three closely related aspects:

1) "the study of nature as knowledge of the truth (*Das Währe*),

2) ethics as the search for good (*Das Gute*),

3) esthetics as the search for beauty (*Das Schöne*)" [DEB 16, section 24]

This very rapid historical development lays the groundwork for more in-depth research that should be conducted in order to understand the evolution of a thought that associates living-beings and knowledge in the same vision. This work goes beyond the scope of this book which will focus more on the recent usage of the concept of ecosystems in terms of the World Wide Web.

To understand the usage of the ecosystem concept, we began monitoring the Web in 2006 up until now and collected 521 documents which we categorized according to 501 keywords. In the following sections, we will analyze this observation through the themes that seem most relevant to us[1].

1.1. For marketing

The first theme we will explore is the most common found online: it concerns the usage of the ecosystem concept in the field of marketing and business. In this context, the linking of a multitude of products or services around a market is represented in graphs that illustrate the concept of the business ecosystem [ASS 16]:

---

1 https://www.diigo.com/user/luckysemiosis?query=%23ecosysteminfo

Figure 1.1. *The advertising ecosystem in Europe*

Keeping in the same field, this next example shows how the term ecosystem is used to illustrate the relationships between different actors and how these actors define strategies for the implementation of a marketing campaign:

Figure 1.2. *Ecosystem of a Web strategy[2]*

---

2 Illustration: https://www.mauricelargeron.com/referencement-socle-d-une-presence-internet/

The final example that we present below highlights one of the limitations of using the ecosystem concept, in that the notion is used here to define a marketing process as well; however, this time, the graphic does not illustrate the complexity of an ecosystem but rather the linearity of a commercial discourse:

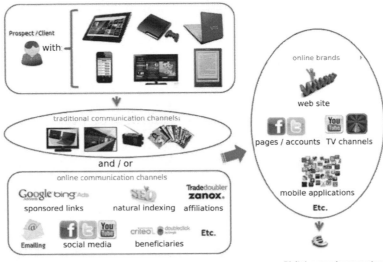

Figure 1.3. *A commercial vision of the digital ecosystem[3]. For a color version of the figure, see www.iste.co.uk/szoniecky/ecosystems.zip*

In Figure 1.3, the ecosystem concept is used only to insist on a multiplication of the elements; however, all the complexity of the processes is blurred in favor of a single type of relation: the production of money.

1.2. For personal data

Another use of the ecosystem concept is the management of personal data and its construction within a space made up of technologies, networks, data and humans. The example below summarizes how an individual is at the origin of a universe of interactions through a "personal cloud". As we can see, the ecosystem of personal data embraces a wide range of inter-connected services where governance forms the basis and the main problem.

3 Illustration: http://www.bricebottegal.com/definition-histoire-web-analytics/

In this illustration, we note that there is no connection that returns to the individual; this feedback loop is nevertheless a fundamental notion of an ecosystem (see section 3.1.3) and even more central to the notion of personal data management. Indeed, how do we give individuals the means to take control of their data without the possibility of reflective manipulation?

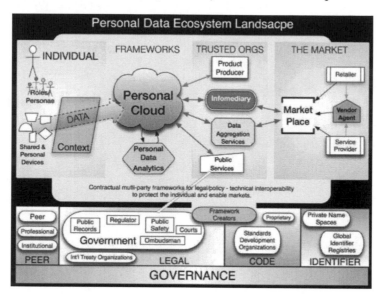

Figure 1.4. *Personal data ecosystem[4]*

The management of personal data and its impact on the construction of a digital identity is becoming all the more important in the current era of the Internet of Things and the quantified self. This is evidenced by the CNIL publication on "the new body as a connected object", and more particularly the section dedicated to the "ecosystem and performance"[5].

1.3. For services and applications

Beyond the business and marketing aspects, the "Web Giants" (Google, Apple, Facebook, Amazon, Microsoft, also known as GAFAM) develop ecosystems through the multiplication of services and applications.

---

4 Illustration: https://image.slidesharecdn.com/2015-ghc-kaliya-151021184700-lva1-app6891/
95/ethical-market-models-in-the-personal-data-ecosystem-31-638.jpg?cb=1445453607
5 https://www.cnil.fr/sites/default/files/typo/document/CNIL_CAHIERS_IP2_WEB.pdf

In order to capture the attention of users, GAFAM deploys a multitude of services and applications whose operation is conditioned with respect to the technical and legal rules of each company. To use these resources, you must necessarily enter the ecosystem of these companies as shown by the popup windows that offer to connect you through your account to a particular company, which thus becomes your identity provider (see section 5.1.2.8).

Figure 1.5. *Ecosystem of Google services and applications*

In the case of Google, there are a hundred services that are available to users and especially developers who, by using them, will hybridize the Google ecosystem in other areas. Therefore, Google will multiply its ecosystem by giving developers the means to build their own niche markets (see section 5.1.2.3). This raises the question as to the accessibility of these ecosystems and their eventual transformation into "walled gardens":

> "From an immense open ecosystem, the Web of today is a succession of what Tim Berners-Lee calls '*walled gardens*', founded on proprietary data and the alienation of their users by prohibiting any form of sharing with the outside. The challenge is no longer simply that of open data, but that of *metacontrol*,

that is, the increased control over the migration of our essential data hosted on the servers of these companies, as a result of the trivialization of *cloud computing*: most of the documentary material that defines our relationship with information and knowledge is about to end up in the hands of a few commercial society" [ERT 11, p. 11].

1.4. For dynamic interactivity

Even if today the dynamic interactivity of a web page seems to be commonplace, it is one of the more important aspects that transforms the Web from a simple document into a living knowledge ecosystem. Since the advent of Web 2.0 and the publication of content that is accessible to all through the simple tools that are social networks, that is, content management tools (see section 5.1.2.9) or services and applications, the Web is teeming with knowledge that is constantly appearing, updating or disappearing. What are totally new in the life cycle of the Web document are real-time updates and the possibility of tracing successive updates. As a result of these two characteristics, we can follow the "pulsations" of the Web as if one is observing a living ecosystem.

For example, the "Listen Wikipedia" web application shows changes to Wikipedia in the form of bubbles that appear and produce a particular sound that is calculated automatically:

Figure 1.6. *Listen Wikipedia*

1.5. For pictorial analogies

In parallel with the conceptual usage of the ecosystem as a notion, discussed above, our observation revealed instances where this notion of using the analogy with ecosystems was used as a model to organize the graphic and thematic presentation of a site or an application.

The simplest usage is the creation of a domain name related to ecosystems, for example, through the notion of a garden, and to simply use this theme to design an editorial line. This is the case, for example, of a site like https://www.opengarden.com/, which sells an application, allowing the sharing of information between several devices. If we cannot argue that the linkage is actually connected to the ecosystem notion, the analogy is not pushed further than the name and a logo. We could multiply the examples of this type of site that make a very basic use of analogy. On the contrary, there are other sites that go a little further in their use of the ecosystem notion, especially those seeking to describe an organization of work. For example, on this website of a Web agency, we find Figure 1.7, which seeks to highlight the aspect of an ecosystem in its approach:

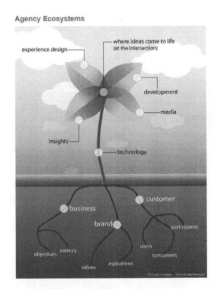

Figure 1.7. *Ecosystem vision of management*[6]

6 http://darmano.typepad.com/logic_emotion/2007/06/agency-ecosyste.html

Figure 1.8. *Ecosystem vision of blogging*[7]

In the same type of use, we find another illustration (Figure 1.8) which explains how the development of a blog is a complex thing that requires different phases of work.

We note that these last two illustrations represent an analogy of the ecosystem given that they use a plant/tree as the core image that is linked to a landscaped context that clearly marks its anchorage in an ecosystem where branches are in contact with the sky and related to the roots that are in contact with the earth. This distinction is important because it makes it possible to not consider all the uses of the tree principle as analogies of the ecosystem. Indeed, even though the hierarchical menu found everywhere on computer screens is probably inspired by a tree structure, this by itself does not correspond to an ecosystem approach.

The analogy of ecosystems is used on the Web not only as fixed representations of concepts, but also in dynamic representations that will "grow" as the image is constructed or viewed:

---

7 https://visual.ly/community/infographic/computers/blog-tree-new-growth

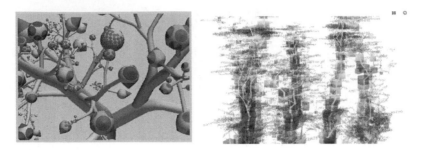

Figure 1.9. *Dynamic representation of the tree*[8]

The example, Figure 1.10, this time shows how to grow an ecosystem forest by proposing that contributors grow trees through the creation of short graphic animations.

The examples we have just presented illustrate how, through data originating from the Web, it is possible to build an ecosystem-inspired representation. It is precisely this analogy that Tim Berners-Lee and Hans Rosling use in their presentation at the TED conference to explain the structure of Web ecosystems and how its future will require the statistical and dynamic modeling of the information environment.

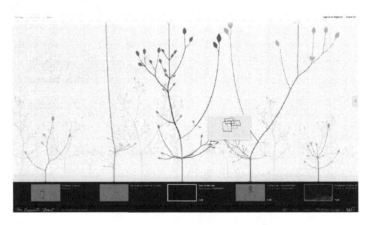

Figure 1.10. *Exquisite Forest*[9]

---

8 http://www.visualcomplexity.com/vc/project_details.cfm?id=37&index=37&domain=, http://www.riekoff.com/tree
9 http://www.exquisiteforest.com/

Hans Rosling: Stats that reshape your world-view
FILMED FEB 2006 . POSTED 2006 . TED2006

Figure 1.11(a). *Analogy of the ecosystem*[10]

TALKS

Tim Berners-Lee on the next Web
FILMED FEB 2009 . POSTED MAR 2009 . TED2009

Figure 1.11(b). *Analogy of the ecosystem*

Regarding the relationship between knowledge ecosystems and biological ecosystems, we should note that beyond the representation of a plant on a screen, the future may lie in the development of tangible interfaces that directly use a real plant as an interface for manipulating information. Technologies that make plants interactive, such as those proposed at the SIGGRAPH '12 conference by the Disney research laboratory [POU 12] or the "EmotiPlant" interface [ANG 15], suggest that this type of interface is not science fiction, and may well appear soon.

---

10 https://www.ted.com/talks/tim_berners_lee_on_the_next_web?language=en, https://www. ted.com/talks/hans_rosling_shows_the_best_stats_you_ve_ever_seen

Figure 1.12. *Example of biological interface: Botanicus Interacticus*

1.6. For the information and communication sciences

In scientific literature, there are many occurrences of the term ecosystem that are used to describe very different contexts. The impact of this notion of an ecosystem in the information and communication sciences (ICS) still needs to be analyzed in detail, but some clues show both an old interest and, for example, the notion of "hypertextual gardening" [BAL 96, p. 170], as recently evidenced by the EUTIC 2015 conference on digital ecosystems or even more recently as part of the call for papers for the conference on "Digital Ecologies" organized by *l'École supérieure d'art et de design d'Orléans*[11]. The status of the ecosystem concept in ICS is still minimal but has the propensity to grow[12].

If we refer to ISIDORE[13], the research platform for digital data in the humanities and social sciences, the term "ecosystem" yields nearly 30,000 results spanning 27 disciplines.

The diagram in Figure 1.13 shows a change in the number of references over time, indicating an increased importance of the notion of an ecosystem with the predominance found in geography that accounts for more than 26% of the total results, whereas ICS represents just under 4%. It should be noted

11 Link to the conference archives: https://hal.archives-ouvertes.fr/EUTIC2015
12 Link to the call for contribution: http://calenda.org/409949
13 https://www.rechercheisidore.fr/apropos, interview conducted on 11 June 2017

that until the 2010s, the notion of an ecosystem in ICS represented barely 1% of the results (about 10 documents). After 2010, however, the percentage increased to reach more than 6% in 2015 (240 documents), which shows an increasingly significant use of the concept in this discipline.

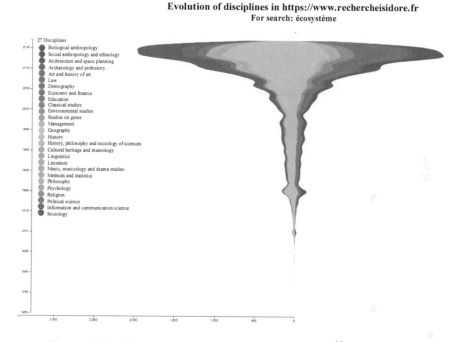

Figure 1.13. *Disciplinary use of the term "ecosystem"[14]. For a color version of the figure, see www.iste.co.uk/szoniecky/ecosystems.zip*

It is, of course, necessary to relativize this evolution in relation to the corpus of the platform which does not correspond completely with the evolution of scientific production in the information and communication sciences [FRO 13], but only to that which was digitized and accessible. As a comparison, here is another diagram that this time shows the disciplinary evolution of the term "hypertext". The predominant discipline this time is the ICS, which represents nearly 22% of the final results for a smaller story that only began in 1983.

---

14 The dynamic and interactive version of the diagram can be found here: http://gapai.univ-paris8.fr/jdc/public/graph/streamv?type=getHistoDiscipline&q=%C3%A9cosyst%C3%A8me

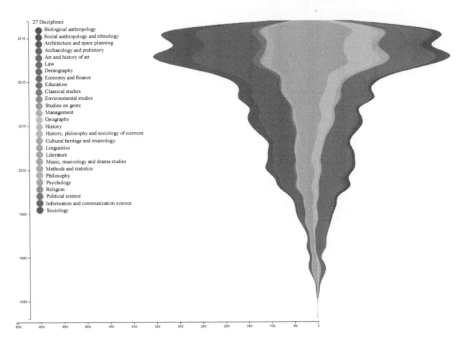

Figure 1.14. *Disciplinary use of the term "Hypertext"[15]. For a color version of the figure, see www.iste.co.uk/szoniecky/ecosystems.zip*

15 The dynamic and interactive version of the diagram can be found here: http://gapai.univ-paris8.fr/jdc/public/graph/streamv?type=getHistoDiscipline&q=hypertexte

2

Ecosystem Modeling: A Generic Method of Analysis

It is argued that
natural logic is full of shadows;
it demonstrates
mathematical logic, lightness.
So who has reason?
The one who seeks what separates them
or the one who seeks what unites them?
J.B. Grize

Complexity saves logic
like a hygienic thought
and makes transgressions
like a thought mutilator.
Edgar Morin[1]

We live in an increasingly complex world whose analysis is also becoming increasingly complex. It can only be envisaged through collectively organizing our intelligence. There are examples of an epistemological framework whose purpose is to guide the researcher in their analysis. The one proposed by A. Coutant and J.-C. Domenget [COU 14] is

---

1 Translation of French quote.

particularly interesting because it is dedicated to scientific investigations of unstabilized phenomena whose fleeting nature recalls the context of an ecosystem. However, we will deviate from this approach. We will look more at the advantages found in the proposals of Mioara Mugur-Schächter [MUG 06] or Pierre Lévy [LÉV 11] whose ambition is at a more generic level. Our purpose is less about the expression of ideas than the algorithmic processing of their symbolic expressions.

In other words, what interests us here concerns less the description of a semantic *terroir*, that is, a sign system whose meaning evolves according to the place and the temporal fluctuations, but rather the modeling of the seeds that will grow in this *terroir*.

To carry out this project, it is necessary to take into account the entire design chain of a computer platform from its interactive design via ergonomic human–machine interfaces to visualization and data processing algorithms and ultimately the database. As noted in [JAT 16], it is a complete ecosystem that must be designed:

> "Via the creation of digital databases in the Humanities and the Social Sciences (HSS), this is a whole research habitat that is taking place whose ecology deserves more consideration." [JAT 16, section 9][2]

The objective of this chapter is to present this ecosystem through the different stages of a collective intelligence platform project for the generic analysis of knowledge. The design work that we present here is spread over 20 years, which we propose to trace here, in order to show how this project has evolved in terms of the different phases of research action.

2.1. Hypertextual gardening fertilized by the chaos of John Cage

When I was working in art history on the influence of the American artist John Cage, I quickly realized that I needed a tool to manage the relationships between artists, works and the opinions about them at different times and in different latitudes. To answer this need, I learned about databases, and more

---

2 Translation of French quote.

specifically modeling aspects, in order to find the right model to manage these networks of influences. At the same time, inspired by the chaotic processes of John Cage and the first reference works on hypertexts [BAL 96], I became interested in the generative dimensions of computing and the possibilities that it offered. Hypertextual gardening [BAL 96, p. 70] has proved to be a very challenging concept to meet information modeling needs as well as a design model for human–machine interfaces (HMIs) required for information retrieval, collation and evaluation.

From these ideas, the design for a collective intelligence platform emerged, and the result of several experiments that would be too lengthy to detail here. It is sufficient to say that these experiments consisted of:

– developing an automatic generator of philosophical text from the random search of a library;

– designing a multi-agent system to evaluate and design an adaptive hypertext;

– creating a knowledge universe through recursive algorithm modeling in 3D fullerenes[3] in the form of galaxies and planets;

– equipping a car with a multimedia system for the spatio-temporal exploration of the cultures of a given territory.

2.2. An entrepreneurial experience

Before finally being called the *Jardin des Connaissances* or JDC (Garden of Knowledge), the collective intelligence platform that we designed was presented to Cap Digital (2006) as part of the first call for competitiveness cluster projects under the name of *Jardin semantique* (Semantic Garden). For this call for projects in knowledge engineering, we described the initial aspects of the platform. To show the timeliness of this project, as far as 10 years later, we will cite the core strategy behind this call for projects and the texts that were proposed in response to it.

---

3 https://fr.wikipedia.org/wiki/Fuller%C3%A8ne

2.2.1. *Objectives*

The objective of this project was to develop a cognitive 3D interface for knowledge management. It was designed to organize both human–machine and machine–machine interactions in the form of a massively multiplayer serious game. Its goal was to connect knowledge within spacetime by modeling a semantic universe that interacted with other semantic worlds.

2.2.2. *Principle of the game*

Just like The Glass Bead Game described by Hermann Hesse [HES 02], the "cognitive garden" aims to stimulate knowledge by showing its organization and its complexity. However, where The Glass Bead Game is for the elite, educated specifically to play and understand the meaning of the game, the one we will propose is for the general public (7 to 107 years). Instead of presenting the information with an abstraction that is difficult to understand, the Cognitive Garden uses the analogy of the garden to make the management of information obvious by drawing inspiration from gardening practices.

We propose setting up an ecological simulation system where the player aims to garden information. Specifically, they must plant seeds, cut and graft shoots, fertilize the roots, make the soil, share resources and choose information flows that continuously feed the growth of plants. The branches represent the texts, the images are the leaves, the sounds are the fruits and the videos are the flowers. The roots will illustrate the conceptual organization of knowledge.

The goal of gardening is to create semantic maps (see section 4.2) using simple graphic gestures: cut, paste, move, deform, color and name. The player will have thus organized a network of interrogations based on a tree-like structure, and by using the Venn diagrams (schematic representation of sets with intersecting curves, see section 4.3.1). From this network, through a continuous exchange process, complex queries are generated and confronted with information flows (Google, Wikipedia, RSS feeds, other cognitive gardens, etc.). We thus obtain a representation of the relationship between a particular problem and a data source which allows us to automatically deduce what must be retained, ignored, proposed, etc.

Throughout its culture, the garden accurately reflects the cognitive ecology of the player. It turns out that the goal of the game is twofold. Besides the interest in everyone to know each other better, the Cognitive Garden also allows for a rich interaction between communicating machines since that is the way to transcribe in computer language what a person knows, wishes and refuses, and therefore to satisfy more precisely their expectations.

2.2.3. Motivations

The control and analysis of information are major issues for a society where complexity continues to grow by increasing the amount of information to manage and the multiplication of interactions with communicating tools. Simple technologies must therefore be put into place so as to make the information available to all.

2.2.3.1. Why model a cognitive ecology?

The whole body of knowledge can be considered as an interacting information system; a cognitive ecology represents this whole body as an ecosystem where types of knowledge maintain an ecological relationship with each other and together form what is called the noosphere (see section 3.1.1).

The Internet is a computer representation of the terrestrial noosphere. Most often, we query this information source via a search engine, which we communicate with on a case-by-case basis through textual queries. Modeling a cognitive ecology makes it possible to envisage the search for information via a process of continuous exchange in real time between a global ecology (the Internet) and a particular ecological niche (the Cognitive Garden). Depending on the characteristics of the ecological niche, the information from the global source will automatically become linked.

The man/machine/machine interaction implemented thus finds its usefulness in a world where the modeling of real-time exchanges between communicating machines is developed with respect to precise and complex uses. A communicating device must react according to the cognitive ecology of the person who uses it; take for example, a tourist in Paris, or a consumer in a store or a job seeker looking for employment, and so on and so forth.

Modeling a cognitive ecology is a way of organizing the complex interactions between individuals and machines in a specific timespace in relation to a universe of knowledge.

2.2.3.2. *The relevance of the garden analogy*

The passage through a symbolic formalization through the use of analogy makes it easier to understand the complexity of cognitive ecology. The garden analogy offers a conceptual framework in relation to an ecology that is coherent, such as the action of planting a seed that is an analogy for the posing of a problem. Another example is the action of cutting a branch that corresponds to the rejection of a specific datum or set of data.

The garden offers a "self-evident" framework for the design and representation of a relationship between information and the territory: what grows on this *terroir* has a particular flavor, a particular form, a different mode of interaction than what grows on the other side of the fence; in the field of information management this means that the meaning of information is conditioned by its territorial context (see section 5.1.1.1). In addition to the conceptual management of space, the garden is also useful for understanding the temporal organization of events. The life of a tree can be seen through the examination of growth rings counted in the cross-section of its trunk, which makes explicit the fact that the production of information varies with time in terms of both quantity and quality (see section 4.3).

The analogy of the garden offers a model for the spatio-temporal representation of information, which is the fundamental basis needed to make sense of something. To illustrate this consistency, here is the analogous description of the interface elements: between the soil and the space, from the seed to the fruit, from the leaves to the flowers, each of these elements interacts with the clouds and the planets.

– planets symbolize and concentrate the story of a real or fictional individual and their relationship with the Earth (Figure 2.1). They are vertically positioned to the planetary location of production of these data according to a distance proportional to the time occupied in this place by the individual; their orbit evolves in parallel with the movements of the production source. The size of the star is proportional to the importance of the data produced;

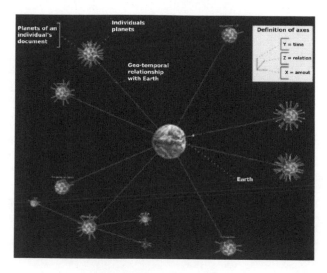

Figure 2.1. *Planet analogy*

– clouds (Figure 2.2) represent the automatic flows that feed the growth of plants. These are news items that provide dynamic and changing content, such as RSS feeds, search engines, services or websites (see section 5.1.2);

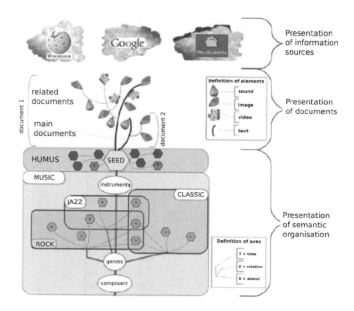

Figure 2.2. *Garden analogy*

– the semantic layers represent the conceptual categories; the oldest are the deepest in analogy with the stratigraphic layers found in archeology. A layer has multiple zoom levels that correspond to the thematic tree. These are organized in a three-dimensional coordinate system where the Y-axis corresponds to the temporal dimension (creation, purchase, birth, etc.), the X-axis corresponds to the importance of the theme and the Z-axis corresponds to the proximity of the themes. The semantic layers are of two natures: either they compose the humus from the semantic elements that the recommendation algorithms have defined or they constitute the semantic *terroir* made from the choices that the user expresses;

– the roots represent the positioning of a datum in the semantic field (semantic layers). Selecting a root activates the data linked to it (vegetation) and *vice versa*;

– the seeds contain the rules of development for the plant, e.g. the organization of the automatic actions of the machine and those that the player will have to carry out to cultivate the plant: take a picture, record a sound, write a sentence, etc. The seed is designed as a partition for the machine and the player. Its function is to define the creation processes of the plant. At this point, we are aligned with what members of OULIPO [BLO 14] did with the literature or John Cage with artistic creation [COL 98];

– the vegetation represents the documents according to their nature, the text corresponds to the branches, the photos to the leaves, the videos to the flowers and the sounds to the fruits. The branches take the title of the organization of the text (chapters, sentences) or else as specified by the user;

– the HMI can use other elements such as a butterfly that grazes the vegetation of the different gardens to create automatic summaries on a given theme and/or fertilize the gardens visited, etc.

The relevance of the garden analogy is also observed in the adequacy between information management processes and gardening practices. These processes are designed to be both manual and automatic. In the case of the latter, the automatic growth of plants is envisaged, for example, according to day/night cycles which cause the roots to automatically grow in the semantic layers of the humus as per algorithmic recommendations in order to open the knowledge to serendipity, that is, the possibilities of finding something interesting when we are not searching for it. In a more manual way, the gardening mechanisms like a cut branch will automatically serve to compose the humus by giving the algorithm recommendations, a setting according to what the user does not want. Similarly, the user's actions to add or modify or delete semantic layers, thereby controlling the roots within them, will provide the settings of what the user wants. Another gardening action can be particularly relevant to the management of information, through the hybridization of several branches in order to observe information and semantic fluctuations. Similarly, planting a branch into particular semantic layers makes it possible to observe the balance between an organization of information and a conceptual categorization.

In short, the Cognitive Garden makes it possible to present the relation between the information (the vegetation) and the semantics of the information (the roots in the semantic layers). The graphical interaction with the data (grafting, cutting, rooting, etc.) makes it possible to generate different types of queries and configurations for the recommendation algorithms. The humus will be the space for algorithm choices, the semantic layers of the choices made by the user. As a result, the Cognitive Garden makes it possible to graphically define a network of questions in continuous interaction with a data network.

2.2.4. Strategic interests and potential benefits

Today, there are efficient communicating machines and programming specifications for their interactions; however, there are no tools available that graphically make sense of this relationship between the producers and users of information. The strategic interest of this project is to propose a simple and global solution to the question of meaning for the usage of communicating machines. From this point of view, two parallel potentialities seem to emerge. On the one hand, the development of an interface for the management of individual, collective, institutional cognitive ecology, etc.: the Cognitive Garden. On the other hand, the professional production of cognitive gardens (seeds, semantic *terroirs*, autonomous agents, etc.) that are intended to be used by communicating machines: tour guides, school programs, trade specifications, among others.

The knowledge management system that we propose is based on a simple and transposable concept, regardless of the user's original culture: gardening. In addition, the global scope of the project, namely to manage the knowledge in the digital and physical spaces and in time (from $-\infty$ to $+\infty$) naturally requires that it adopts a European and global scope. The following is a non-exhaustive list of business opportunities that can be considered with the Cognitive Garden:

– business intelligence services for key accounts;

– cognitive gardens on particular themes in partnership with stakeholders in the fields of: tourism, education, marketing-advertising-commerce, etc.;

– advertising on websites using the Cognitive Garden technology;

– software extensions to develop the garden.

2.3. The maturation of a research project

Since the semantic garden project did not find partners that were important enough to support its development in the context of a start-up or a company, we continued to develop it as part of a university research program to refine theoretical bases and ergonomic perspectives. This work took the form of an ICS thesis [SZO 12c] and several scientific articles [SZO 10, SZO 11a, SZO 11b] wherein we revealed the fundamental principles for the modeling of an informational existence in a knowledge ecosystem. We will present these principles later in this book (<u>Chapter 3: Fundamental Principles for Modeling an Existence</u>). These principles have evolved, as research is refined and experiments have been made to validate conceptual and technical solutions.

2.3.1. *Evaluating index activity*

One of the first experiments that we conducted was the development of an algorithm to represent the semantic layers of a folksonomy built using the Web Delicious[4] application. The objective was to evaluate the indexing activity of a person or a group of people such as a student promotion. In addition to the technical problems posed by the choice of technologies, we came up against challenges of interoperability and computability of tags. For the technical questions, we quickly made the choice of a client–server architecture based on a MySQL database (see section 5.1.3.6), which is driven by PHP services, and a client application built from the XML language dedicated to the definition of vector graphics: SVG (see section 5.2.4.1.2). Concerning the challenges regarding the semantic management of

---

4 https://del.icio.us/luckysemiosis

tags, it appeared to us that we needed a pivotal language that would allow for the translation of tags into natural language in order to increase their computability. The choice of language is oriented towards IEML (see section 4.1.2), whose semantic addressing principles offer good perspectives for both semantic interoperability and the graphical representation of these addresses.

From these tag translations in IEML, we have developed algorithms to translate these semantic addresses into dynamic and interactive graphs. To facilitate the use of these algorithms and the comparison of different visualizations, we have set up a tool to dynamically configure them and to thus quickly explore the available data. The parameters for the algorithm are broken down into five sets.

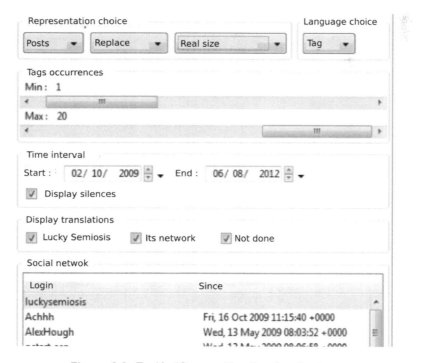

Figure 2.3. *EvalActiSem: setting the visualization*

With this interface, it is possible to change the representation parameters in order to change the type of graph displayed. We will only show here the graphs that represent the temporal succession of "posts" in Delicious[5] in the manner of "archeosemantic layers" which gradually pile up, one above the other in chronological order, from the oldest at the bottom to the most recent at the top (Figure 2.4). The last two display parameters concerning the size of the representation are real (Figure 2.4) or compressed (Figure 2.5).

Finally, the choice of the language of the tags makes it possible to display the tags as they have been typed or their IEML translation. The next step is the filtering of the data parameters, defining the intervals of the minimum and maximum cooccurrences and/or the time ranges to be taken into account. We can also specify if we want to see display periods where no action has been made (silence). The following parameter acts as a translation dashboard in order to know which ones have been made and by whom. Finally, the last parameter allows us to choose the social network of the connected user, the individual for whom we want to display the indexing activity.

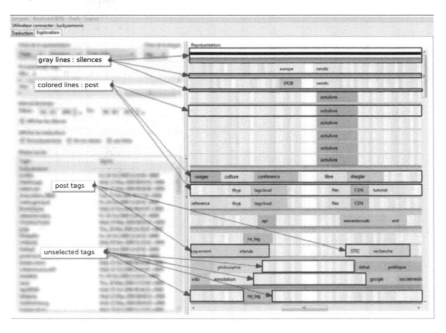

Figure 2.4. *Archeosemantic layers. For a color version of the figure, see www.iste.co.uk/szoniecky/ecosystems.zip*

5 A "post" in Delicious corresponds to the registration of a series of tags for a URL.

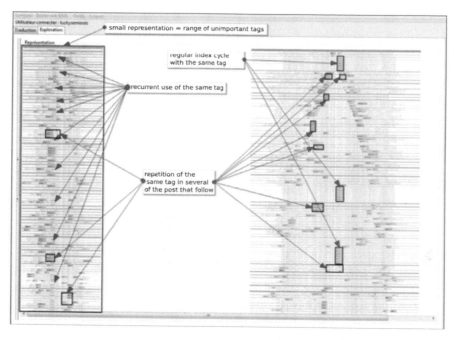

Figure 2.5. *Comparison of two users. For a color version of the figure, see www.iste.co.uk/szoniecky/ecosystems.zip*

This application offered the possibility of putting one representation next to the other two representations so as to compare, at a glance, the semantic activity of two users. The screenshot in Figure 2.5 shows, for example, that the user on the right uses a smaller variety of tags than the user on the left, since their representation is less broad. The representation for the choice of tags over time offers many possibilities for the interpretation of semantic activity. We note that, on the right, a recurrent cycle of the same tag corresponds to a regularly recurring activity. This can be linked, for example, to receiving the latest information on a fixed date. On the left, we see a strong recurrence of the same tag which probably indicates the interest of the author in a particular theme. Yet another example, in both graphs, we observe a repetition of the same tag in posts that follow each other, which could signal an indexing activity that tends to focus on the same theme in the course of the same Internet search.

2.3.2. *Folksonomies explorer*

This experiment jointly conducted a technical problem, involving exploring the graphical possibilities of JavaScript Protovis[6] library, predecessor to the D3.js library (see section 5.2.4.2.2), and a theoretical problem, which reflected on the readability of the information in Big Data. Indeed, the calculation of the visualizations is now accessible in real time through a simple Web browser. To give a visual representation of the data, there is no need to install specific software or to have a particularly powerful machine. The Web provides both technologies and data. Let us examine through a specific example, how it is possible to model representations and provide the user with the means to navigate Big Data.

The multiplication of data makes it more and more difficult, if not impossible, to consult it. Even while conducting experiments on a computer with a high performance index (5.9)[7], we encountered difficulties in visualizing representations calculated using a Delicious folksonomy when containing too many entries. Despite the size, range of occurrence, and date filters we added to address these issues, some visualizations could not be saved or even displayed onscreen. The solution to this problem is to explore the data by multiplying the interactions with graphical states.

The general principle is equivalent to a space wherein each step executes a reconfiguration, each representation being like an individual point of view within a landscape of data. Technically, this space is a hypertext whose nodes, anchors and links are dynamically calculated according to the potential representation (virtual) and the choice of the user (actual). As a representation of a space, this hypertext has a cartographic dimension that makes exploration processes such as zooming and moving the background map (refer to section 4.2). We have implemented these two processes to visualize data in the form of bubbles (Figure 2.6). These navigation possibilities are however limited, especially when there are too many data or the representation model does not support them. Therefore, we looked for other ways to represent the data in order to facilitate the exploration thereof.

---

6 http://mbostock.github.io/protovis/
7 For a definition of the performance index, visit: http://goo.gl/Ucyxf

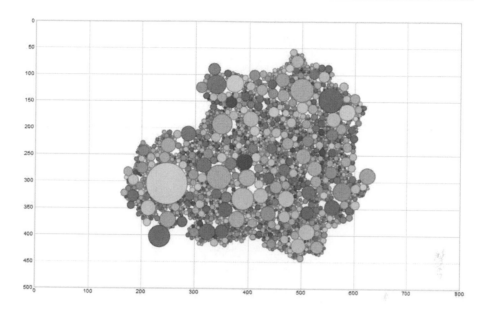

Figure 2.6. *Cloud of bubbles from a folksonomy*

To experiment with these new possibilities, we will take the example of the "DHYP" tag used by five teachers from the Hypermedia department at Université Paris 8. The scenario which we propose is the most detailed exploration of the data possible, without being impeded by problems associated with performance or data readability. For this, we follow the most global approach, that is, from the author of the annotation to the most detailed, that is, the tag.

Let us begin by suggesting that the user chooses which authors will be taken into account for the visualizations. In this case, the number of authors is relatively small, and we used a Venn diagram to graphically model one of the 30 possible permutations of the five authors following the recommendations of Jérôme Thièvre in his thesis on mapping information searches:

"The Venn diagram formulation is superior to textual formulation, because it makes structural errors related to the parenthesis of Boolean expressions impossible, and avoids problems related to the misinterpretation of the semantics of Boolean operators. Indeed, the meaning of Boolean operators AND and OR is sometimes confused with the meaning of the coordination conjunctions AND and OR of natural language. Thus, the disjunctive operator OR is frequently interpreted as exclusive. The conjunctive operator AND is sometimes interpreted as a union rather than an intersection." [THI 06, p. 33][8]

Rather than choosing, via several clicks, a selection form composed of checkboxes, it appears more ergonomic to allow the user to choose with a single click in a Venn diagram:

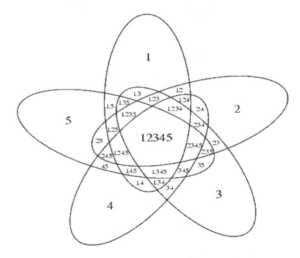

Figure 2.7. *Venn diagram selection form*

To make this diagram interactive, we initially vectorized each element of the above graph manually with Inkscape[9] software, indexing it with an identifier corresponding to one of the 30 permutations: v_1, v_1_2, v_1_2_3, and so on. Thus, we were able to coordinate the elements of the graph through a particular semantics, for example, to filter the tags in relation to the authors who use them: v_1 = single author 1, v_1_2 = authors 1 and 2, etc.

---

8 Translation of French quote.
9 https://inkscape.org

We then developed an algorithm in the form of a web service that creates a table with the number of tags that a group of users has in common compared to the cooccurrences of a tag. The data we obtain allows us to build a website in two parts (Figure 2.8). On the left, the Venn diagram allows for the update of the right part by clicking on an element where the colors of the graphic elements correspond to the number of occurrences of the permutation. To make this diagram dynamic and interactive, we use the following algorithm.

For each permutation:

– construction of the identifier and the wording of the SVG element;

– recovery of the SVG element;

– deletion of the default style if it exists;

– calculation of the color using the Protovis library;

– changing the color of the element according to the number of links;

– adding update events from the right side.

esterhasz et fennec_sokoko : 11 TAG(s)

Figure 2.8. *Venn diagram: example of interaction*

The Venn diagram works like a compass that semantically locates a range of data. To do this, the background color of the element is automatically changed to green. In parallel, a datum can be located in the coordinate system organized by the diagram. We design each diagram as an existence in an ecosystem. For example, an event on one chart affects other diagrams and *vice versa*. However, in the example we present, this interaction is only in the direction from global to detail. Events on a parent chart cause changes on a child diagram and *vice versa*. For an update of the "detail-child" to the "global-parent", it is necessary to set up functionalities for the modification of the raw data. In our case, the raw data is always the same, only the visualization data changes. Therefore, there is no retroactive loop on the raw data, as is the case in a natural ecosystem where any modification of an existence has repercussions on other existences.

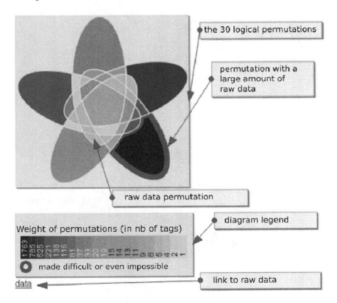

Figure 2.9. *Venn diagram for the selection of permutations*

To explore the raw data we generated, here are the rules we adopted in the visualization engine:

– Venn diagram: this presents the entire data subdivided into 30 permutations (Figure 2.9);

– the representation of one of the distributions with respect to the three dimensions (Figure 2.10):

– the number of times or a cooccurrence between two tags is used;

– the number of times the tag is used;

– the number of documents associated with a tag;

– the filtering of raw data for each element of the three dimensions.

Clicking on one of the elements in one of the three dimensions causes the raw data to filter against that element. By default, all data are displayed except for permutations with too many data (red outlines). In this case, only the first three elements of each dimension are displayed.

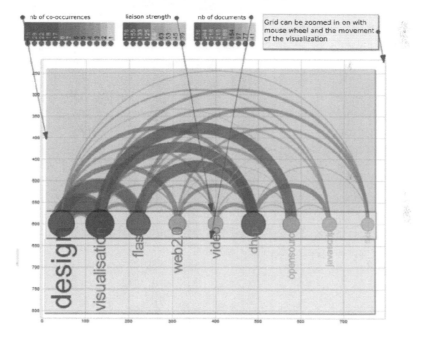

Figure 2.10. *Data filter interface*

This visualization scenario is one of many examples of what can be done to allow a user to explore a body of data and make sense of it through generative rules for constructing an interpretation. The design of visualizations increasingly tends towards the provision of a "potential" representation or, to put it another way, the objective is to model a virtual network. In this context, a visualization becomes the reality of a virtuality, the designer is thus tasked with defining the visualization parameters, the user with choosing which of these constraints will be updated. Therefore, the job of the designer is to define a network of perspectives in which the user chooses a particular point of view. In this sense, the interpretation of a piece of information is conditioned in the first place by the designer, who models the amplitude of potentialities, and in the last instance by the user, who chooses the various visualization parameters.

2.3.3. *Tweet Palette: Semantic mapping*

As part of an information design workshop given to students of the French Master 2 THYP and the Pro CDNL[10] degree, during the 2011–2012 academic year, we asked students to pool their information development and graphic designer skills in order to create an interactive semantic mapping that makes it easy to send tweets during a conference. The idea was to have a palette of concepts, just as painters have a palette of colors, in order to quickly express an interpretation. In this context, we conceive of semantic cartography not only as the representation of an information space from structured data [TRI 06], but also as the provision of a system of conceptual coordinates for positioning information within a semantic space.

Particular acknowledgment must be given to the intervention of Raphael Velt, who presented his work around Polemic Tweet[11]. The five groups of students created maps that allow, with a simple click, building a tweet corresponding to the interpretation of an event during the course of a conference (Figure 2.11). Following this work with the students, we have implemented such a mapping from a Scalable Vector Graphics (SVG) graph (see section 5.2.4.1.2) and some lines of JavaScript code. On the contrary, making generic and interoperable concepts used in the semantic space defined by these cartographies is much more complex and as a result rarely implemented.

---

10 Link to the training site: http://www.humanites-numeriques.univ-paris8.fr/-LP-CDNL
11 http://polemictweet.com/

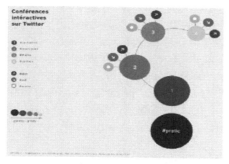

http://goo.gl/OXXVa

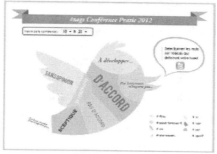

http://goo.gl/6nTLo

Figure 2.11(a). *Tweet Palettes made by students*

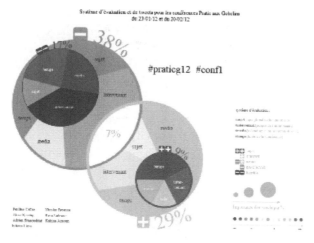

http://goo.gl/BsQQQ

Figure 2.11(b). *Tweet Palettes made by students*

According to the Information and Communication Modeling Model we use (Chapter 3: Fundamental Principles for Modeling an Existence), an interpretation is the expression by an actor of a relationship between a design and a document. Developing an application for the interpretation of an event consists of managing these four dimensions: actor, document, report and design. Before dealing with the issue of design management through a semantic map, let us take a look at how we handled the dimension of documents and reports in the Tweet Palette web application.

On the Web, the easiest way to refer to a document is to give its address as a Uniform Resource Locator (URL). We chose this way to inform the documentary dimension of our application. Due to lack of time, we have not developed a more complete interface to view the document being interpreted nor even align the content of a video or stream sound in line with the conceptual coordinates. For the moment, the reference to the document is limited to a web address that the author of the interpretation must enter in the form dedicated for this purpose. The application is therefore very flexible, because the interpretation can relate to any document on the Web. In this sense, the application is very close to folksonomy editing tools like Delicious or Diigo.

What also brings about the application of folksonomy tools is the fact that the connection between a document and a concept is carried out by an actor who has authenticated himself. In our model, this actor is considered as the generator of reports – in other words, it is he who creates the relationship between the document and the concept. Here too, the choice we made for managing actors is extremely simple. Indeed, we developed only two formulas: the first to create a user account and the second to authenticate. In the future, it would be desirable to use tools dedicated to this management function (see section 5.1.2.8). In any case, what matters to us, in this application, is the ability to identify the information related to an actor and, if necessary, compare how several actors adopt different or similar points of view. Once the management of the documents and the users was set up, we devoted ourselves to what we believed was the most important aspect of this work: how to manage a layer of semantic information starting from a system of conceptual coordinates.

As part of the framework on information design, we came across a visualization by David McCandless[12] that is particularly well adapted to our problem. Indeed, this "information designer" brings together a collection of general concepts to evaluate the quality of ideas and create a taxonomy for them. The author positions the concepts in a system of coordinates organized with respect to a vertical axis scaling the strength of the conceptual structure, a horizontal axis graduating the functionality of an idea and the origin for these two axes corresponding to the absence of an idea. In addition, the axes are enriched with concepts that specify the graduation and define the semantic spaces at the intersection of the vertical axis and the horizontal axis. With this coordinate system, the designer places concepts corresponding to the semantic spaces defined by the axes, e.g. the concept of "abstract" is at the meeting of the concepts of "dysfunctional" (horizontal axis) and "harmony" (vertical axis). In the context of a public event such as a conference, this can be used to interpret the lecturer's speech as the ideas are presented.

To make this visualization interactive, we opted for a generic solution, whatever the representation applicable. To do this, we developed an algorithm that adds an interactivity layer to a static representation by taking into account the semantics of this one. The principle of this application is very simple. It consists of placing the representation into an HTML container and then attaching an event reciever to this container that reacts to a click and finally to interpret, through an algorithm, the relation between the position (x, y) of this click and a conceptual matrix that creates consistency between the graphical and conceptual coordinates.

With this application, a click on a graph makes a precise location in a semantic space possible by producing the coordinates of this space. For example, the following expression, produced by the application "56#super - 40#trans 11#harmonic -77#synthesizing #great", specifies that the click is located on the horizontal axis, graduating the functionality of the idea between "super" and "trans", while on the vertical axis, it measures the conceptual framework of the idea between "harmonic" and "synthesizing".

---

12 http://www.informationisbeautiful.net/visualizations/a-taxonomy-of-ideas/

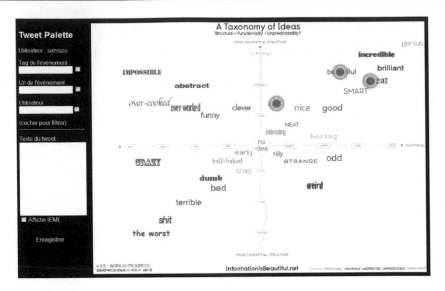

Figure 2.12. *Tweet Palette*

It is obvious that the design choices and their relative position are from the author's perspective of the graphic and another author may have a different point of view. To this end, David McCandless's proposition must be considered as the cartographic projection of his subjectivity within the global semantic space of the noosphere. Even if this projection is only the expression of a point of view, that is, a map and not a territory, because of it we are able to situate an idea and compare the position of this idea in relation to others.

As already stated, one of the problems with per-word indexing is the interoperability and computability of natural language (see section 4.1). To solve this problem, Pierre Lévy proposes through IEML a language to map knowledge ecosystems by considering them "at the core of a coordinate system that would make its transformations describable through computable functions"[13] [LÉV 11, p. 62]. The goal is not to limit the meaning of a single representation that makes the mistake of taking the map for the territory [BER 09a, p. 188, LEL 09], but to the contrary, to stimulate a "creative conversation" [LÉV 11, pp. 89–111] from precise and unambiguous information about the designs used and the points of view and inflections that the participants in the conversation wish to express.

---

13 Translation of French quote.

To evaluate the feasibility of such a project, we have enriched the conceptual grid of our application with a translation of the concepts in IEML. Therefore, we can provide, for each concept used in David McCandless's map, a semantic address that corresponds to our understanding of this design. For example, we translated the horizontal axis of the map through the following IEML expression: [E:A: .M:M:.-su-su-'E:.- 'E:U:A:.-',], which means:

– [E:A: .M:M:.-] for "horizontal axis";

– [s.u.-s.u.-] for "idea";

– [E:.-'E:U:A:.-',] for "functional cause".

This translation work today is still relatively tedious since there are no tools that can assist the user in this task yet. However, the effort needed to find the right dictionary terms and adequate articulations is very beneficial for improving the understanding of the concept and to better understand its semantic space. Moreover, as a regular language for the construction of a topology, IEML makes it possible to evaluate semantic distances to calculate, for example, the projection differences among several different interpretations. There is still work to be carried out in a future version of the application[14].

---

14 For a more detailed presentation of this application, see [SZO 12d].

3

Fundamental Principles
for Modeling an Existence

Everything in life
had condemned us to have
but inadequate ideas [...]
The first adequate idea
that we have had,
is the notion of commonality.
Gilles Deleuze

The mind develops knowledge
by working between
[an absolute known as it is] and
[an absolute forever beyond our knowledge],
but from which one develops
descriptions that are communicable
and inclined to intersubjective consensus.
Mioara Mugur-Schächter[1]

We have just presented some of the experiments that have been conducted to evaluate the relevance of the Knowledge Garden (KG) and consolidate the technical specifications that we will detail below (see section 5.2). This practical development has also enabled us to refine the theoretical principles that are at the heart of this ecosystem modeling platform, including the key concepts that are used when reflecting upon ecosystems:

---

1 Translation of French quote.

the Spinozist proposals for an ethical ontology [DEL 01]; the ontological matrices of Philippe Descola [DES 05]; and the reflexive continuum inspired by Pedauque [PED 07]. We will first present the key concepts used in the contemplation of knowledge ecosystems before proposing a method for the modeling of information existences within these ecosystems.

3.1. Key concepts for thinking about knowledge ecosystems

In the field of information and communication sciences, and more generally, in the reflections affecting the organization of knowledge, we have identified the key concepts used by contemporary researchers following a scientific approach that uses the concepts of "ecosystem" and "ecological principles".

Whether we follow Augustin Berque, Francis Chateauraynaud who recalls the need for an "ecology of discursive practices" [CHA 15, section 53] to lead socio-computer surveys, or Yves Citton who insists on the ecological dimension of attention [CIT 14], or many other researchers, all seem to follow the slogan of Bruno Latour: "Between modernizing or ecologizing, we must choose."[2] [LAT 12, p. 13]

3.1.1. *The noosphere*

Pierre Teilhard de Chardin was one of the first with Édouard Le Roy and Vladimir Vernadsky [GRI 16] to use the term noosphere in order to describe this "collective mind" with a spatial metaphor whose laws for the sharing of our reflexivity and the development of collective intelligence remain to be discovered:

> "A harmonized collective consciousnesses, equivalent to some kind of supreme consciousness, with the Earth not only filled with innumerable grains of thought, but enveloping all by a single thought, to the point of functionally forming one vast Grain of Thought at a cosmic scale. A plurality of individual ideas gathering and iterating into a single act of unanimous reflection."[3] [DE 97, p. 203]

---

2 Translation of quote from https://entitleblog.org/2015/06/27/fifty-shades-of-green-bruno-latour-on-the-ecomodernist-manifesto/.
3 Translation of French quote.

Beyond the mystical dimension of this definition and its anchoring in Jesuit thought [JOS 11, p. 36], other authors, such as Gaston Bachelard, have also used this term to describe "the sphere of thought" [BAC 10, p. 217], like Gregory Bateson's "the ecology of the mind" [BAT 08] or Edgar Morin who gives a definition of the noosphere in terms of an ecosystem:

> "The noological sphere, constituted from all the phenomena known as *spiritual*, is a very rich universe which entails ideas, theories, philosophies, myths, fantasies and dreams. [...] These are not 'things of the mind'. They are the life of the mind. These are beings of a new type, informational beings [...] they are able to multiply by drawing the negentropy from human brains, and, through them, from the culture that feed them; our minds and more broadly our cultures are ecosystems in which they find, not only sustenance, but serendipity."[4] [MOR 81, p. 340]

With the emergence of digital technologies and the Internet, the noosphere has shifted states from a speculative concept to that of a tangible reality, to the extent of Marshall McLuhan's view that the noosphere has become "the technological brain of the universe" [JOS 11, p. 38] and that the Web is a dynamic and interactive representation of this noosphere:

> "Teilhard de Chardin termed the 'Noosphere' as the global ecosystem of all ideas through the globalization and development of the means of communication and which converge and which we begin to touch upon in cyberspace."[5] [LÉV 03].

With the proliferation of this "layer of evolutionary complexity even faster and more creative than that of organic life" [LÉV 11, p. 61], there is practically no information that escapes this technological noosphere, which leads to the transformation of work into "intelligent cooperation of minds connected via networks" [MOU 10, p. 66]. Therefore, parallel to our physical and biological environment, a symbolic universe develops from which emerges "conceptual ethologies" [NOY 10, p. 198] that we must understand and analyze.

---

4 Translation of French quote.
5 Translation of French quote.

On this point, we join Yves Citton who clearly marked his positions for the need to analyze this noosphere:

"Describing society as 'a web of interspiritual actions and mental states acting on each other' is by no means an idealist bias [...], but it simply points to one being engaged in 'thinking about human reality through the attribute of Thought' rather than that through extension."[6] [CIT 08, p. 49]

In this, he joined the definitions of Teilhard de Chardin in assimilating the intellectual technologies to a collective brain governed by laws that we have yet to invent at the border between sociology, psychology and economy:

"This system of 'mental states scattered among a large number of separate brains', and which forms these states by governing their processes of interconstitution, will have to be explained in terms of production, exchanges, competitions and flows. In short, in terms which treat this system as an economy: the 'collective brain' [...] is a good illustration of this *oikos* in which the mental acts of a human population are invited to 'get along well', according to the laws (*nomoi*) of production, transformation and interaction, and which belong to the sociologist-interpsychologist-economist to formulate."[7] [CIT 08, p. 53]

3.1.2. *Enaction*

To continue our exploration of the key concepts necessary for an ecosystem approach, let us present the notion of enaction that Maturana and Varela defended in a book that has since became famous: *The Tree of Knowledge*. This notion refers to:

"An approach to knowledge which places at its center the idea that meaning emerges from the interaction of history with a biological system."[8] [MAT 94, p. X]

---

6 Translation of French quote.
7 Translation of French quote.
8 Translation of French quote.

The basic idea of these two authors is that the object and the subject of knowledge are two sides of the same process and that both are mutually specific. As Yannick Prié remarks in his HDR[9] [PRI 11], in referring to this notion, the mutual specification between the subject and the object is also at work in the "information space" resulting from an "interactional coupling" with the user. As a result, the emergence of meaning is not predicted, but rather emerges from self-poiesis and self-organization, another key concept of Maturana and Varela.

Due to their dynamic and interactive capabilities, digital interfaces can be considered as biological systems whose interactions with the user bring out meanings and, over time, knowledge. The visualization of this process, the skills pool that it generates and their analyses are undoubtedly what motivated the experiments for the trees of knowledge [AUT 99, AVE 13], and which remain one of the drivers behind the thought of Pierre Lévy, notably through the concepts such as the ecosystem of ideas and the ecosystem of algorithms [LÉV 11] (see section 4.1.2).

3.1.3. *Complexity*

How can we not cite this concept that has been the foundation for much thought over decades and which is at the heart of ecosystem issues? We owe this great method work to Edgard Morin, who has made the concept of complexity, the synthesis of nature [MOR 81], of life [MOR 85], of knowledge [MOR 92], of ideas [MOR 95], of humanity [MOR 01] and of ethics [MOR 06]. By showing how, in any field, analysis gains openness and precision through the integration of dialogic, recursive and hologrammatic principles, Edgard Morin gives us the means to think about the multiplicity of interactions and the richness of a fundamentally living knowledge.

By the term dialogic it is necessary to understand:

> "The complex association (complementary/competing/antagonist) of instances, which together necessitate the existence, operation and development of an organized phenomenon."[10] [MOR 92, p. 98]

---

9 "*Habilitation à Diriger des Recherches*" is a French qualification, allowing the individual to carry out university teaching.
10 Translation of French quote.

Similarly, the recursive principle corresponds to:

"A process where the effects or products are, at the same time, causers and producers of the process itself, and where the end states are necessary for the generation of initial states."[11] [MOR 92, p. 101]

The hologrammatic principle is a type of organization where:

"The whole is in a certain way included (engrammed) in the part that is included in the whole. The complex organization of everything (*holos*) requires the registration (engram) of everything (hologram) in each of its individual parts; therefore, the organizational complexity of everything requires the organizational complexity of its parts, which requires a recursive organizational complexity of everything."[12] [MOR 92, p. 102]

These constitutive principles of the complex approach give us a complementary conceptual framework to those we will present later for the modeling of knowledge ecosystems.

3.1.4. *Trajective reason*

Augustin Berque explores human environments through questions that emanate from geography, history, social sciences and ecology. Through this practice, which he calls "misology", he proposes a theorization of the fundamental dynamics that are at stake in the ecumene:

"The ecumene is a relationship: the relationship to both ecological, and the technical and symbolic humanity of a given land. It is therefore not limited to the materiality of physical being [...], nor that of its human population [...]. The ecumene, it is necessarily this, but also not necessarily the least, the existential expansionism that exists in each human being, and which has always exceeded the geometrical definition of the body."[13] [BER 09a, p. 17]

---

11 Translation of French quote.
12 Translation of French quote.
13 Translation of French quote.

At the heart of the mesological approach, the trajective reason is, for Berque, a means of going beyond "modern objectivism" by making the approach to knowledge more human through an "existential pulsation" between an intelligible external world that is discovered through technique and a sensible inner world that we explore through symbols. He summarizes this operative concept with a formula:

> "The body and the world, through the earth and through the flesh, are the unit of human existence (lgP/lgS) and the ecumene (lgS/LGP), in the structural moment of their mediance: (lgS/lgP)/(lgP/lgS)."[14] [BER 09a, p. 402]

3.1.5. *Agency*

The concept of agency, popularized by Alfred Gell [ALB 17], comes from the desire of researchers to break away from Western paradigms and the epistemology that they convey through binary oppositions such as those between Nature and Culture, Object-Subject, Form-Essence, etc. Rather than considering a supposedly unique world, these researchers explore their field according to the principle of a multitude of ontologies and experiences that allow us to define, in a variety of ways, the categories of people, of living beings and things. These different ontologies are brought about through agents considered as material artifacts capable of weighing on the actions exerted within the societies by the "affordances" of the substances that compose them, namely, their latent potentialities.

From this concept, we will retain the idea that the agent as an artifact is "thinking material" that participates in the same way as the user in the co-design of the act:

> "Making, then, is a process of correspondence: not the imposition of preconceived form on raw material substance, but the drawing out or bringing forth of potentials immanent potentialities in a world of becoming. In the phenomenal world, every material is such a becoming, one path or trajectory through a maze of trajectories." [ING 17, section 15]

---

14 Translation of French quote.

The agency concept is particularly interesting when substituted into the evolution of computer development techniques. Indeed, the history of computer coding practices shows how computer scientists changed their coding practice as the data being managed became more and more complex. They went from simple scripting to object-oriented programming, then on to multi-agent systems, and finally to ecosystems such as those of GAFAM (see section 1.3). In this context, we observe how computer coding tends towards ever greater code agency in terms of both autonomy and interaction with an environment.

Another way of conceiving interactions in cognitive ecosystems in terms of agents is proposed by Yves Jeanneret, through the concept of "cultural being" which he defines as follows:

"A set of ideas and values that embodies a cultural object within a society by constantly transforming itself through the circulation of texts, objects and signs."[15] [JEA 14, p. 11]

It would probably be necessary to deepen this connection between "cultural being" and "agency" in order to show to what extent these two concepts combine with the third: the "power to act" [BRU 17].

3.2. Spinozist principles for an ethical ontology[16]

Let us examine how in the 18th Century, Spinoza brought some interesting reflections useful in the consideration of the nature of information to the table, the means of managing it and how our relationship to ubiquitous information via the Web can be compared with the relationships that the 17th Century thinkers entertained when considering divine omnipresence. This comparison today is all the more relevant to the development of a vision for a Web with divine attributes [SZO 10], or as Bernard Stiegler said in commenting on the works of Gilles Deleuze and Félix Guattari:

"The abstract machine, like a machine with infinite memory, is only a mathematical formalization of the attribute of God to metaphysicians."[17] [STI 05, p. 220]

---

15 Translation of French quote.
16 This chapter is inspired by [SZO 12C].
17 Translation of French quote.

In this sense, the metaphysical reflections of the modern era provide us with simple bases of understanding that allow us to better analyze our own relationship with information, but also not to neglect the spiritual dimension always present in a global approach to knowledge management.

3.2.1. *Spinoza: ethical ontology*

We have developed the first principles of this reflection in collaboration with Philippe Bootz. As part of a project for the archiving of digital poetry [BOO 08], we were inspired by the Spinozist ontology to model the power of a poetic work to act. The goal is to design a web application to keep track of the interpretation of a work by different actors instead of archiving only the physical dimension of this work, which in many cases is not possible, for example, ephemeral works such as installations or due to the very lability of the digital works. In this sense, we follow Bruno Bachimont who remarks that:

> "The true complexity of heritage conservation lies in the fact that it is not enough to simply safeguard objects, but rather we must also preserve their understanding so that they remain capable of being revived, not exactly, but [...] in terms of an interpretive continuity."[18] [BAC 07, p. 236]

This research on ontological modeling from Spinoza's propositions has its roots in these interpretations by Gilles Deleuze [DEL 68, DEL 01, DEL 03]. From these references, it seemed obvious to us that Spinoza's project to elucidate on the ethical and ontological relationship resonated fully in the field of ICS at a time when ontologies become norms for the organization of information and where ethical issues (identity, use, law, etc.) focus as much on the concerns of users as on the attention of researchers.

> "A Spinozist recognizes himself in the most basic form as being in this curious position: ethics and ontology are according to him one and the same thing."[19] [RAB 10, p. 32]

---

18 Translation of French quote.
19 Translation of French quote.

3.2.2. *Limitations of Spinozism*

Of course, we must question the limitations of the Spinozist principles that were after all developed in another era and in another context, different to that of ICS, as David Rabouin reminds us that the relevance of Spinoza should not make us forget the limitations of his approach:

> "By refusing the reduction of the body to a univocal determined form of the extension [...] This separates us from the happy time when we could still believe in an unequivocal regime and homogeneous description of reality."[20] [RAB 10, p. 32]

However, when the field of application of this Spinozism is the Web, which precisely possesses this unequivocal and homogeneous reduction of reality in the form of 0's and 1's, the relevance of Spinoza is all the more obvious. This does not mean that the Spinozist vision of the Web tends to make it unambiguous. On the contrary, the formal uniformity of the Web in a Spinozist vision brings coherence to the understanding of what is at stake in a world of plurivocity. The example of folksonomies is very enlightening here [LIM 10]. Since users share a uniform code with the same interfaces in order to categorize homogeneous resources in the form of a URL, it is possible to recognize a different point of view among the many others. In Spinozistic terms, we could say that in the face of these same extensive parts (Web resources), different relationships are expressed through a link to a key word (tag) and it is the essence of these points of view.

Hence, the question that arises is about the possibility of standardizing not only the means of expressing a point of view, but also the very expression of this point of view. On this point, Spinozism provides us with a useful insight assuming the fact that, whatever the formal precision that we can give to the "coding" of knowledge, it will not allow us to transcribe the entire learning experience; something which Rabouin recognizes with a beautiful frankness:

> "This was the mistake of my youth: to believe that we could reform Ethics, make it more 'rigorous', by drawing inspiration from the logical formalisms that have flourished since the late 19th Century. Since the recourse to 'formalisms' only overshadows the problem posed by the use of mathematics and

---

20 Translation of French quote.

that of perfect adherence (or so-called) of the experience (be it that of figures or symbols) to the 'concept' or to the 'form'."[21] [RAB 10, p. 62]

This shadow inherent to the relationship between form and knowledge occupies the center of the diagram that represents the model we adopt (Figure 3.1). This is the place that is reserved for the creation of relationships, that which is occupied by the human or by the machine. In the case of the machine, the shadow can be partially lifted by the designer who will develop in a computer language the instructions and implement the algorithms for linking the information. However, in the case of the Web and complex algorithms, there will always remain a part that is obscure, because no one now completely masters the various information layers through which information passes; either because of the necessary technical skills or because these layers are not publicly accessible, and ultimately due to the incompleteness of "computational reason" [PAR 16]. What can be said about the user who has no idea of the circuit that passes along the information between his click and the display of data and who without being able to read computer code essentially finds himself in the situation of Jean-François Champollion without the Rosetta Stone. For this individual, the machine is a black hole that works as if by magic. The same goes for its own functioning and its ability to adhere its knowledge to a concept or a form. How many of us are able to unveil this connection between form and knowledge? Does not a part always remain obscure to us?

3.2.3. *Three dimensions of existence and three kinds of knowledge*

Deleuze describes the Spinozist proposition in the form of an ontology composed of the three dimensions of existence:

"Therefore the three dimensions, the external extensible parts from one to the other and which belong to me, the relations through which these parts belong to me, and the essence as well as degree, *gradus* or *modus*, of the singular essence which is expressed in these relations."[22, 23]

---

21 Translation of French quote.
22 Translation of French quote.
23 http://goo.gl/LLJ3g

In parallel to these three dimensions of existence, Deleuze explains that Spinoza associates the three kinds of knowledge:

"– Inadequate ideas and passions, refer here to the dimension of existence, to the first dimension: to have extensible parts.

– The other two aspects, knowledge of the ratios and knowledge of the degrees of power, as intensive parts, refer to the two other aspects: the characteristics of relations and the essence as an intensive part."[24]

The first kind of knowledge consists of affects, which Spinoza calls "inadequate knowledge". In his opinion, this knowledge results from the simple encounter (shock) between the extensive parts of the two individuals in a given time and place. Deleuze takes the example of splashing to illustrate this knowledge: the encounter with the wave is purely sensual and emotional:

"Splashing around is simple, it indicates this well, we see that these are extrinsic relations. Sometimes the wave smacks me, and sometimes it takes me away. That is the effect of shock. It is these shock effects, that is, I do not know anything about the relations that are constituted of or that break them down, I get these effects from extrinsic parts. The parts that belong to me, are shaken, receive a shock effect from the parts that belong to the wave."[25]

For the first kind of knowledge, this knowledge is of the effects of the contact between entities. On the contrary, the second kind goes deeper into the knowledge of the event:

"The second kind of knowledge is the knowledge of relations. Of their composition and their decomposition."[26]

This second kind of knowledge should not be reduced to its abstract dimension of which mathematics is "the formal theory". This knowledge leads to know-how, which makes it possible to compose the characteristic

24 http://goo.gl/wWIsr. Translation of French quote.
25 http://goo.gl/IVp9X. Translation of French quote.
26 http://goo.gl/IVp9X. Translation of French quote.

relationships that an individual maintains with its extensive parts and those of another individual, so that contacts are no longer reduced to a simple shock between extensive parts but maintain a composition of relationships between the parts. Gilles Deleuze takes the example of swimming to illustrate this second kind of knowledge and demonstartes that this knowledge is not abstract:

> "What I mean to say: my characteristic relationships, I know how to compose them directly with the relationship of the wave. It does not pass between the wave and I, that is, it does not pass but between the extensive parts, the wet parts of the wave and the parts of my body; it passes between these relationships. The relationships that make up the wave, the relationships that make up my body and my ability when I know how to swim, to present my body in the relationships that make up directly with the wave relationship."[27]

Swimming illustrates how an activity in which the relationships that I maintain with my limbs are composed in relation to the relationships that the essence of the wave maintains with its molecules. It is the knowledge of these essences which constitutes the third kind of knowledge:

> "The third kind of knowledge or intuitive knowledge is what? It goes beyond relationships and their composition and decomposition. It is the knowledge of essence. It goes beyond relationships, since it reaches the essence that is expressed in relationships, the essence upon which relationships depend."[28]

Through this modeling of knowledge-existence, what Jean-Max Noyer called "onto-ethologies" [NOY 10] is the expression of a simple organization of information that allows us to deepen our model of an informational existence. The following diagram shows the three dimensions of existence correlated with the three kinds of knowledge. The ambition of this diagram and this reading of Spinoza is to pose hypotheses concerning the existential management of knowledge.

---

27 http://goo.gl/IVp9X. Translation of quote from http://www.scielo.br/scielo.php?pid=S0104-12902015000500027&script=sci_arttext&tlng=en.
28 http://goo.gl/IVp9X. Translation of French quote.

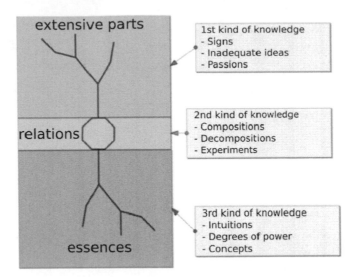

Figure 3.1. *Spinozean principles of information – communication*

Expressed in this form, we can clarify our model of informational existences by insisting that the extensive parts compose one of the dimensions and therefore inevitably condition our access to knowledge by anchoring it within spacetime. All knowledge necessarily passes through a physical dimension in the form of a contact with other bodies whether as a wave or a particle. However, the relation between the dimensions of existence and the kinds of knowledge leads us to deduce that these extensive parts that make up symbols inevitably convey inadequate ideas:

> "The conditions in which we know things and are conscious of ourselves condemn us to have only inadequate ideas, ideas that are confused and mutilated, effects separated from their real causes."[29] [DEL 03, p. 30]

Therefore, we can consider the management of knowledge as the experimentation here and now of the relationship between an individual's extensive parts and essences. It follows from our model that the extensive parts correspond to a physical dimension related to a time and a place. The first kind of knowledge consists of coming into contact with this physical dimension, but without knowing what it means or even what its use is. The

---

29 Translation of quote from http://www.situation.ru/app/j_artp_901.htm.

transition between the first and the second kind of knowledge involves recognizing that this physical dimension is related to a contract of meaning passed on through other individuals. The transition to the third kind of knowledge consists of interpreting the meaning of the contract. However, the whole problem of knowledge according to Spinoza is to remove oneself from the inadequate ideas of the first kind in order to access the second and third kinds of knowledge:

"This is precisely the problem: each individual has three dimensions (of individuality) at the same time, however, there are individuals who will not leave the first kind of knowledge. They do not rise to the second or third. They will never be able to form what Spinoza calls a 'common notion', a common notion being precisely, as you will recall, 'the idea of a relationship'. The idea of a characteristic relationship. All the more, they will never have knowledge of their singular essence or other singular essences."[30]

3.2.4. Spinozist symbol politics

The Spinozist vision of an ontology-ethics that combines existence and knowledge shows how much the manipulation of knowledge ultimately involves many other issues in addition to the technical management of information. We will have the opportunity to come back to this, but let us first emphasize the political dimension of information technologies and the inherent dangers in these practices. The Spinozist information organization model provides us with a tool to evaluate this practice in relation to the kinds of knowledge and the dimensions of existence that must be mobilized in order to manipulate symbols.

Every individual has the three dimensions of existence; however, they do not necessarily have access to the three kinds of knowledge. It is the individual and collective experiments that will enable him to access "here and now" the different types of knowledge. However, the developments in artificial intelligence and digital social networks are most often based on a vision of collective intelligence similar to that of insect societies. For reasons of technical feasibility, we only consider the first type of individuals' knowledge, that of shocks via pheromones. We recall that the ideal of a

---

30 http://goo.gl/IVp9X. Translation of quote from http://www.scielo.br/scielo.php?pid=S0104-12902015000500027&script=sci_arttext&tlng=en.

Spinozist society, according to Gilles Deleuze, is opposite to that of an insect society since it excludes the duty to obey:

"The best society, then, will be one that exempts the power of thinking from the obligation to obey, and takes care, in its own interest, not to subject thought to the rule of the state, which only applies to actions. As long as thought is free, hence vital, nothing is compromised. When it ceases being so, all the other oppressions are also possible, and already realized, so that any action becomes culpable, every life threatened."[31] [DEL 03, p. 10]

This vitalistic vision of thought and knowledge is reflected in Spinoza by a rejection of the symbol that inevitably involves a relationship of order and obedience:

"For Spinoza in the field of knowledge, any symbolic relationship is absolutely excluded, driven out, eliminated [...] if there is a symbol domain, it is that of the order of command and obedience."[32]

The smallest coding experience with a computer language shows just how accurate this point of view is. Computer coding makes it obvious that symbolic languages have unmissable commands. It is impossible not to obey the orders of the syntax, e.g. to forget a ";" or to insert too large a space; the slightest fault renders the code no longer viable. However, beyond these formal commandments which belong to the first kind of knowledge: that of inadequate ideas; there exists the composition of relations in the rules of computer language, the understanding thereof makes it possible to reach the second kind of knowledge. If we understand that putting a ";" allows us to specify that an instruction is finished, we pass from the first kind of knowledge to the second one. We pass from strict obedience to an order, to an understanding of the compositions of relations (of links) in play within this computer language that requires a strict separation between the instructions. From then on, we will not be subjected to the rule, but instead we will allow for the one who acts upon this rule, to express the composition of relations. On the contrary, if the understanding of the compositions of relations is absent, only the original composer will compose the knowledge, which in the Spinozist model will lead the individual to adopt a moral point of view:

31 Translation of quote from http://projectlamar.com/media/Deleuze-Spinoza-Practical-Philosophy.pdf.
32 http://goo.gl/7MlS0

"Even the technical rules take on a moral aspect when we ignore their meaning and only retain one sign."[33] [DEL 68, p. 49]

Hence, in situations where a computer does not work or a web page does not load due to an error, individuals confined to the first kind of knowledge will be able to exclaim: "This machine is mean, it is angry with me!" Note that this behavior from the point of view of the machine may very well be faced with an institution or a society whose laws it does not understand. The knowledge will therefore consist of the individual's understanding of the compositions of relations involved in order to no longer be subjected to them through a moral lens that judges right and wrong, but to act on these relations through an ethical lens that favors what is good at the expense of what is bad:

"The law is always the transcendent instance that determines the opposition of values for Good-Evil, but knowledge is always the immanent power that determines the qualitative difference of modes of good–bad existence."[34] [DEL 03, p. 37]

3.2.5. *Spinozist ethics for the Web*

At the root of the Spinozist approach, that which can be considered important is the place of the individual in relation to information. Between revelation and expression, the individual is differentiated by the way in which s/he adopts information between "subjected to" the command of the sign and "acts" on the essence of the signified:

"Never was there as much of an effort to distinguish two domains: revelation and expression. Or two heterogeneous relations: that of the sign and the signified, that of the expression and the expressed. The sign is always attached to a particular thing; it always means a command: and it forms the

---

33 Translation of French quote.
34 Translation of quote from https://books.google.co.zw/books?id=SeNLAQAAQBAJ&pg=
PA21&lpg=PA21&dq=The+law+is+always+the+transcendent+instance+that+determines+the
+opposition+of+good-bad+values,+but+knowledge+is+always+the+immanent+power+that+
determines+the+qualitative+difference+of+the+good-bad+ways+of+existence&source=bl&ots=
ONCZ-uQmgh&sig=SRrvRPDn9jBXTzkB5WQOFuZ3zSk&hl=en&sa=X&ved=0ahUKEwil8v
LmmZbYAhWKJ8AKHQg7BvQQ6AEIJTAA#v=onepage&q=The%20law%20is%20always
%20the%20transcendent%20instance%20that%20determines%20the%20opposition%20of%2
0good-bad%20values%2C%20but%20knowledge%20is%20always%20the%20immanent%20
power%20that%20determines%20the%20qualitative%20difference%20of%20the%20good-bad%
20ways%20of%20existence&f=false (p. 21).

base of our obedience. The expression always refers to an attribute; it expresses an essence, that is, a nature in the infinitive; it makes us know it."[35] [DEL 68, p. 48]

Spinoza's information theory cannot be separated from the use of information where the individual confronts a "way of being", a "mode of existence" [LAT 12]. Following this relationship between information theory and usage, the use of an individual in relation to information as per the dimensions of existence and the kinds of knowledge mobilized is broken down. We have shown with the previous diagram (Figure 3.1) how to represent the organization of these different levels. The following diagram shows an example of this organization with an example of the categorization of a Web resource by a tag:

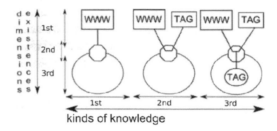

Figure 3.2. *Spinozist information circuit*

This diagram shows how the Spinozist model of information proposes a circuit that starts from the extensive parts, passes through the relations, resonates in the interiority of essences, to formalize relations with new extensive parts. A Spinozist ethics of the Web would be for each individual to position themselves in relation to this diagram by becoming aware of the degree of knowledge and existence that they express by way of being on the Web. Moreover, this diagram can serve as a minimal typology for classifying information on the Web according to the dimensions of existence and the kinds of knowledge that they make available.

3.2.6. *The ontological principles of Descola*

To model informational existences in a knowledge ecosystem, we refer to the ontological principles founded on the anthropological research carried out by Philippe Descola [DES 05], which is presented by Michel Serres thusly:

---

35 Translation of French quote.

"I received a third happiness from destiny. By drawing four archipelagos, Philippe Descola recently classified human cultures. In this way he saved my last folly: I could imagine exploring mankind."[36] [SER 09, p. 7]

In this chapter, we present the ontological principles and, more particularly, the notion of an ontological matrix that produces four types of ontology. We will show that one of these types, the analogical ontology, is particularly well adapted to the Web and to our conception of informational existences. Our intention is not to analyze how these propositions could be criticized, especially in the case of naturalism, which finds its limits in a purely philosophical exemplification [BAB 10, p. 30] or the ambition to want to go beyond the relationship between nature and culture [LAT 15, p. 30], but rather to show how Philippe Descola's propositions bring pragmatic solutions to the question of modeling knowledge-existences which, as an "analogist figuration", aim at restoring "the fabric of affinities within which real or imaginary entities are inserted and thus acquire an agent-like quality" [DES 10, p. 165].

3.2.7. Principles of ontological matrices

Philippe Descola proposes with ontological matrices "the equivalent of a sketch of the painting of Mendeleyev in the field of the symbolic" [BES 06], for this he relies on a definition of ontology which takes as one of its principles that the apprehension of existence depends on the relationships that an individual maintains between interiorities and physicalities.

By the term *interiority*, it is meant that:

"A range of properties recognized by all humans and covering in part what we usually call the spirit, the soul or the conscience – intentionality, subjectivity, reflexivity, affect, ability to signify or dream."[37] [DES 05, p. 168]

We note that the term "moral" was chosen to explain the work of Philippe Descola in the panels of the exhibition *La fabrique des images*, "The Factory of Images", at the museum of primitive arts[38]. For our part, we interpret this term of interiority more as an "ability to signify" or as the "soul" due to its

---

36 Translation of French quote.
37 Translation of French quote.
38 https://goo.gl/8FDY1j

proximity with Leibniz's proposals concerning the "fabric of the soul" as a screen that models the power of discerning individuals.

The concept of physicality is defined by what "concerns the external form... it is the set of visible and tangible expressions that take the specific provisions of any entity when they are deemed to result from the morphological and physiological characteristics intrinsic to this entity." [DES 05, p. 169]

The objective of Philippe Descola through this definition of ontology is to show how the ontological practices of individuals can be analyzed according to the resemblance and the difference between interiority and physicality.

"If only for reasons of cognitive economy [...] there are no more than four ontologies, each organized according to the continuities or discontinuities that humans identify between themselves and the rest of the existing ones."[39] [DES 10, p. 13]

The characteristics defined by these two poles (interiority and physicality) and these two types of relationship (resemblance and difference) form a matrix of four cases which each represent a particular ontological point of view: animism, totemism, culturalism and analogism [DES 05, p. 176]. The principles of this ontological matrix are represented by the following diagram:

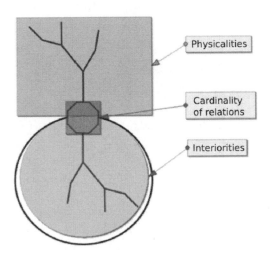

Figure 3.3. *Ontological principles of Philippe Descola*

---

39 Translation of French quote.

In relation to the Spinozist model that we have defined in section 3.2.3, physicality by its external and visible characteristics corresponds to the extensive parts which we know compose the first dimension of existence. In the same way, Descola's definition of interiority is of particular interest to us given that it has the "ability to signify" which is close to the third kind of knowledge-existence: essence. This confirms the following definition of interiority:

> "More abstract notions, such as the idea that I share with others the same essence, the same principle for action, or the same origin, sometimes objectified in a name or an epithet is common to us."[40] [DES 05, p. 169]

Still in this attempt to show the similarities between the Spinozist model and that of the ontological matrices, we note that the notion of relationship or relation which forms, in Spinoza, the second kind of knowledge-existence, is not exclusively an order of intellectualism for Descola:

> "The relationship is therefore not understood here in the logical or mathematical sense, that is, as an intellectual operation allowing the internal connection between two bodies of thought, but in terms of these external relationships between beings and things that can be identified through typical behavior, they are more likely to be partially translated into concrete social norms."[41] [DES 05, p. 164]

This definition corresponds to the notion of relations that Gilles Deleuze describes by insisting on the dimension that is not necessarily mathematical. Notably, he gives as an example of the second kind of knowledge, the practice of knowing how to swim, that is, he establishes the relations between what constitutes a swimmer and what constitutes water.

One of the important points of Descola's theory of "ontological matrices" lies in the fact that it is possible to create a graphical representation as we have shown in Figure 3.2. We can go a little further in the representation of this theory by using the principles of cardinality implemented in relational databases. The two entities whose relations we have to manage are the physicalities and the interiorities. These maintain relations which are either

---

40 Translation of French quote.
41 Translation of French quote.

of the order of resemblance or of the order of difference. Taking the principle of cardinality "1" for the resemblance and the cardinality of "n" for the difference, it is possible to construct Table 3.1.

This principle of cardinality allows us to graphically compare different approaches to a given question as Dominique Boullier showed in the *Entretiens du nouveau monde industriel 2010*, "Interviews of the New Industrial World 2010"[42]. Above all, this principle of cardinality makes it possible to define graphical construction rules as per the preferred ontological approach. We will not detail each of these approaches, instead preferring to focus on the analogical ontology that is most in line with our purpose. Nevertheless, in terms of information, here is how Philippe Descola summarizes the other ontological types.

Ontologies	Diagrams	
Animism : n-1		physical difference
		similar interiority
Totemism : 1-1		physical similarity
		similar interiority
Naturalism : 1-n		physical similarity
		different interiority
Analogism : n-n		physical difference
		different interiority

Table 3.1. *Cardinalities of the ontological matrix*

---

42 http://amateur.iri.centrepompidou.fr/nouveaumonde/enmi/conf/program/2010_2

First, animism is defined as:

"The generalization to non-humans of a human-type interiority combined with the discontinuity of bodily physicalities, therefore provides perspectives on the world and ways of living in it."[43] [DES 06, p. 177]

Totemism is based on:

"The sharing within a class of existence that groups together humans and various kinds of non-humans through a limiting set of physical and moral qualities that the eponymous entity is deemed to embody to the highest degree."[44] [DES 06, p. 180]

Finally, naturalism is:

"The formula of naturalism is the opposite to that of animism: it is not by their bodies, but by their minds that humans differentiate themselves from non-humans, they also differentiate themselves, through their spirit, in groups, as a result of the diversity of achievements that their collective interiority allows to be expressed through different languages and cultures; as for the bodies, they are all subject to the same degrees of nature and cannot be singled out and differentiated according to the various *genera* of life, as was the case in animism."[45] [DES 06, p. 178]

3.2.8. *The Web as analogist ontology*

The appearance of the digital document has upset the attitudes towards the practice of documents and the resulting knowledge, to the point of bringing out a second modernity that Igor Babou analyzed in his authorization to direct research [BAB 10] and that Pédauque defined as follows:

---

43 Translation of French quote.
44 Translation of French quote.
45 Translation of French quote.

"The aim of achieving the totalization of knowledge and the triumph of scientific authorities would be defeated: the second modernization introduces the requirement of reflexivity, a knowledge that declares itself and which is controlled by knowing its limits and its conditions of production."[46] [PED 06, p. 4]

Faced with this evolution of documents and their practices, Pédauque proposed overseeing the emergence of a "post-modern condition, in competition with modern normality" [PED 06, p. 9]. There is much to say about the concept of postmodernity, especially concerning the actuality of J.-F. Lyotard's propositions [LYO 79], his overcoming of hypermodernity [LIP 06], his critique [GUA 89a, pp. 53–61] or the impact on contemporary epistemology of Marcel Duchamp's aesthetic propositions, of which his art piece of the urinal as a founding technique of postmodernity [DE 89] still sheds light on the practice of knowledge in the digital age. However, this would take us beyond the subject of this book. We note, however, that the transition between modernity and postmodernity can be summed up by the passage from a linear vision of historical evolution, where the old must be surpassed in order to produce the new, towards a chaotic vision where the old and the contemporary mingle to create the potentiality of a creative cycle. Between the modernist position of an "already done" history that seeks performance and that of a "making history" postmodernity that privileges creation, we find the same kind of ambivalence as between the symbol and the analogy. The symbol proposes sequences from a fixed "image", whereas the analogy sets up a dynamic network more favorable to the imagination:

"The logic of imagination is not a logic that extracts the conceptual sequences of images; but rather a logic that relies on differences and similarities in the imagination to deploy the network of inferences."[47] [RAB 10, p. 76]

It is therefore interesting to note that the final diagnosis of J.-F. Lyotard concerning the computerization of companies here sheds a particularly relevant light:

---

46 Translation of French quote.
47 Translation of French quote.

"It [the computerization of companies] can become the 'dream' instrument for the control and regulation of the market system, extended to knowledge itself, and exclusively governed by the performance principle. It inevitably involves fear. It can also serve the metaprescriptive of discussion groups by providing the information they most often lack in order to make informed decisions. To follow the fork in the direction of the latter, the path to take, in principle, is very simple: the public should be allowed free access to memories and data banks."[48] [LYO 79, p. 107]

Indeed, the strict control of a symbolic logic that functions in a univocal relationship between form and concept tends to orient our digital societies towards the performativity of an insect society. In order to direct our digital societies to other paths, we recommend that they be conceived from the perspective of knowledge ecosystems, where the relationship between form and concept can be multiplied through an infinite number of perspectives. However, this potentiality of an "n-n" relation between form, concept and individual is exactly what the analogist ontology proposes.

It will be noted that digital information ecosystems already offer this multiplication of the relations between form and meaning by challenging designers with a double complexity corresponding to the two poles (physicality and interiority) of ontological matrices:

"The digital nature of documents requires computer scientists to deal with two complexities: a 'semantic' complexity that corresponds to the fact that the information arrives *a priori* without hierarchy: a 'semiotic' complexity arising from the fact that the methods for the composition of documents, hence the presentations of information, are multiplied."[49] [PED 06, p. 18]

Faced with the connection between these two complexities, we are in a situation where, by its creative plurivocal potentiality of individuation, "the status and the place of analogy and associationism are decisively enhanced" [JUA 10, p. 34]. Indeed, the analogy makes it possible to think of a constantly moving information space where only interactions with the individual make it possible to stabilize:

---

48 Translation of French quote.
49 Translation of French quote.

"The information space is thus, at any moment, the result of the history of its interactional link with the user, which as we know does not have to be optimal, only viable. Each of these equilibria described as stable must also be thought of as metastable, that is, in a dynamic of perpetual change, continuously capable of switching to new emerging equilibria, new tasks, schemas, structures, tools, etc."[50] [PRI 11, p. 82]

This proximity between the ecosystems of knowledge and the analogical ontology is also pointed out by Raphaël Bessis who recognized the fertility of Philippe Descola's proposals when reflecting on the complexity of our hyperconnected societies:

"The advances made by Philippe Descola on pattern recognition, that is analogism, are now more than ever likely to be a fertile source for the understanding of this 'global collective-world' that is being formed in front of our eyes, and by a little more each day, takes the form of a chaosmos of singularities which calls vertiginous self-reflection interpretations, fractal thoughts, analogical cosmologies."[51] [BES 06]

What the analogist ontology proposes is the possibility of creating a "weaving of knowledge" based on a connection between the experiences of everything:

"Each thing is special, but one thing can be found in each thing that links it to another, and that thing to another, in such a way that all worldy experiences are interwoven though the chain of analogy."[52] [DES 10, p. 165]

The similarity of this analogist interwovenness with knowledge ecosystems consists of the "meta"-informational dimension of the analogist process corresponding to a folksonomic practice of categorization:

---

50 Translation of French quote.
51 Translation of French quote.
52 Translation of French quote.

"The ontological schema that it aspires to portray is even more abstract than what other figurative modes seek to objectify: not a relationship of subject to subject, as in animism, or a shared relationship of inheritance with a class, like totemism, or a relationship of subject to object, as with naturalism, but rather a meta relationship, that is to say an all-embracing relationship made up by structuring heterogeneous relations."[53] [DES 10, p. 165]

But where the folksonomic practice is lost in an anarchic relationship of documents, concepts and individuals, the passage through the analogy represented by an allegorical figure provides a framework for creating a strong coherence between the disparate elements:

"Analogy is a hermeneutical dream of completeness that stems from an observation of dissatisfaction: taking note of the general segmentation of worldly components at a scale of small differences, it cultivates the hope of weaving these weakly heterogeneous elements into a web of affinity and meaningful attractions with all the appearance of continuity."[54] [DES 05, p. 281]

And it is from this network of correspondences that analogism will allow an "interpretative journey" [DES 06, p. 182], consisting of a flow of information that operates through a feedback loop between the physicalities and the interiority through an individual's bias.

3.2.9. *Principles of computer models*

This chapter is devoted to the principles of computer models and, more particularly, to the epistemological limits of the symbolic languages from which they are constructed. These are the limits that will define the extent to which we are able to model knowledge ecosystems, that is, to stay within the bounds of what Pierre Boulez called "the fertile country" [BOU 89], by using a technique where the user does not lose his power to decide on behalf

---

53 Translation of French quote.
54 Translation of French quote.

of the machine for its own betterment. We will approach the borders of this fertile country by first tracing a historical connection between ancient Greece and the present era, from Zeno to Turing, and then we will examine the limits revealed by the attempts to write a book in a perfect language.

3.2.10. *From Zeno to Turing via Spinoza*

Let us begin by recalling Zeno's Paradox by borrowing from Deleuze, the words of this story:

> "Achilles will never catch up with the tortoise, said old Zeno, that is ancient Zeno, or, more to the point the arrow will never reach its target. The arrow will and will never hit its target, this is Zeno's famous paradox, given that one can assign half the trajectory, from the arrow's starting point to the target as being half of this trajectory; when the arrow is at this halfway point, there is still a half remaining; you can further divide this half in half when the arrow is at that point, and there is still a half remaining, and so on and so forth. Continue to halve the half and one will always have left an infinitely small space, the small space that always exists between the arrow and the target. The arrow itself has no reason to reach the target."[55]

Is it not the same with knowledge? Like an arrow pointed at a target, knowledge is a movement that symbols divide into steps. With each symbolic trace, we approach to the target, but we also create the conditions of new knowledge and the potentiality of new paths. Thus, symbolic languages endlessly divide knowledge.

> "Therefore the logic which, since its Greek origins, found its place within the rigor of mathematical demonstrations, meets in this same place an internal limitation brought about by its privileged instrument: the letter for this logical expression."[56] [GAU 01, p. 119]

---

55 http://goo.gl/3fbtV. Translation of French quote.
56 Translation of French quote.

At once both wonderful tools for reflection as well as for the construction of knowledge, symbolic languages also carry within themselves this internal limitation linked to the logic and formal system from which Edgar Morin draws two fundamental lessons. The first posits the limitation of knowledge as a principle:

– "an explanatory system cannot explain itself;

– a principle of elucidation is blind unto itself;

– what defines cannot be defined by oneself."[57] [MOR 95, p. 187]

The second lesson is based on the discoveries of Gödel and Tarski. This proposes the opening through a passage to a meta-dimension:

> "Thus, Gödel and Tarski together show us that any conceptual system necessarily includes questions that can only be answered outside this system. The result is the need to refer to a metasystem in order to consider a system."[58] [MOR 95, p. 188]

This point is fundamental because it constitutes an absolute limit to computer modeling and involves a double difficulty that can be summarized as follows:

> "The first difficulty is the combinatorial wall: in cases a little bit complex, the skein of possibilities can never allow itself to be fully unwound in the confined space of machines."[59] [GAN 93, p. 68]

> "The second difficulty is the intrinsic limit of symbolic systems: [...] if it is possible to evaluate consistency and the completeness of a symbolic system when what it designates is formalized, what happens when what it designates is not?"[60] [GAN 93, p. 69]

Despite this double difficulty, we have created hypercomplex symbolic systems with computers that today constitute information ecosystems and whose study has given rise to a deeper reflection on the epistemological

57 Translation of French quote.
58 Translation of French quote.
59 Translation of French quote.
60 Translation of French quote.

limits of symbolic languages. These questions are notably borne by studies on cognition that place themselves in the Gordian Knot that is the calculability of the mind:

"Is the mind computational? In short: does the brain, if we accept the inseparability of the body–brain–spirit, function in its various activities as a machine processing symbols? If the answer is positive, then two consequences are necessary: on the one hand, we have managed to penetrate the enigma of the apparent body-mind duality, which today is one of the most discussed points in philosophy of the mind; on the other hand, we will build an intelligent machine. If, *a contrario*, the cognitive sphere was not computational, would it still be possible to account for it 'scientifically'?"[61] [WAN 05, p. 33]

If we accept the hypotheses put forward in our analysis of Spinoza's propositions, the inseparability of the body–mind–spirit is indeed a characteristic of individuals who are all composed of the three dimensions of existence (extensive parts – relations – essences). In the hypothesis that the brain functions as a symbolic machine, it would be that which causes the relations to reach the second kind of knowledge. However, as suggested above, symbolic languages are confined to this second kind of knowledge by virtue of their formal dimension. Therefore, to the question that arises about the body–mind–spirit relationship, we can answer that indeed the body, the mind and the spirit are indissociable; nevertheless, we must not mix these dimensions of existence with the kinds of knowledge to which they are linked. It is probably possible to conceive of the mind as a symbolic machine, but it does not necessarily follow that the mind is computational and that it functions through the manipulation of symbols:

"Unfortunately, most cognitive science is based on the distorted view that this relatively recent cultural invention [systems of mathematical symbols] is the fundamental architecture of cognition. [...] It is a mistake to think that thinking is, in general, the manipulation of symbols ("Material Anchors for Conceptual Blends", *Journal of Pragmatics*, 37, 2005, 1 575)."[62] [RAB 10, p. 74]

---

61 Translation of French quote.
62 Translation of French quote.

Such experiments, which aim to establish a general knowledge base for an average human being, confirm the limits of this computational approach, because despite the scale of this project, many problems persist:

"Approximately 600,000 categories were identified, described using 2,000,000 axioms. Unfortunately, there is still the question of exploiting this knowledge in order to build theories (implantation of abduction techniques), which theories would be used for prediction (implementation of deduction techniques)."[63] [WAN 05, p. 48]

Our hypothesis is that the third kind of knowledge, that of intuition, composes the inner space of the cognitive sphere, the one that, beyond formal relations, creates the instantaneous resonances of a "decisional fold"[64]. Therefore, we place ourselves after the work carried out in the field of affective sciences that explore the relationship between cognition and emotion by refusing the dissociation between body and mind. Above all, they question "the idea that formal logical laws are directly implemented in the human psyche" [SAN 08, p. 58].

Indeed, it seems possible to scientifically treat the conditions of appearance of formal relationships and even to model the membrane of a cognitive sphere in the form of a "fabric of the soul". This amounts to conceiving what we can also call an economy of affects [CIT 08]. On the contrary, it is impossible to predict the consequences caused by these chaotic processes [GLE 99, LEA 98, CHO 94] within this sphere:

"If, in the state of our imperfect knowledge, we have no reason to suppose that one combination takes place over another, although in reality these combinations are made up of so many events that may have mathematical probabilities or unequal possibilities, and if we mean by the probability of an event the relationship between the number of combinations which are favorable to it, and the total number of combinations put forward by ourselves along the same line, this probability can still be used, for want of better, to fix the conditions of a wager, of any random-walk; but it will cease to express an actual subsisting and objective relationship between things; it will

63 Translation of French quote.
64 http://goo.gl/VArh8

assume a purely subjective character, and may vary from one individual to another, according to the extent of his knowledge."[65] [COU 43, p. 438]

Or to put it in a more poetic way:

"A throw of the dice [...] never [...] will supress [...] chance."[66] [MAL 98, p. 465]

Therefore, the automatic calculations are certainly very useful to define an average, but they are only the reflection of a formal point of view, as shown by the experiment undertaken by Fabien Gandon as part of research based on conceptual distances. This experiment consisted of automatically calculating the value of the conceptual distances "with respect to the proximities naturally felt by humans"[67]. However, the conclusion is particularly tasty, "a structure of subsumption alone does not allow simulating such behaviors"; as conveyed by the name of the chapter in which this experience is recounted and which suggests that the human being would be much less civilized than the machine: *Les distances à l'état sauvage*, "Distances in the wild state".

In fact, symbolic languages produce rigid and fragile systems that cause unresolved problems. The following list makes it possible to understand the extent of this:

"(1) human beings are able to generate new primitives when confronted with new objects; this ability and the problems raised by an alphabet that is not learning, represent a major problem for symbolic modeling;

(2) the essentially symbolic and serial nature of processing information within this type of approach makes models particularly subjective to combinatory explosion and therefore difficult to apply outside the universes and microworlds in which they have been defined;

---

65 Translation of French quote.
66 Translation of French quote.
67 http://goo.gl/GPCk7

(3) in a symbolic system, symbols, in spite of their systematic interpretability, are not anchored; their meanings are parasitic in the mind of an interpreter;

(4) sensory information about the physical world is always assumed to be digital (light intensities, forces, frequencies, etc.). Therefore, there should be at least one non-symbolic computational layer between the real world and the paradigm of pure symbols;

(5) taking into account uncertainty is not obvious."[68] [WAN 05, p. 31]

The whole of these points can be summed up in the question which includes all of them, namely the fact that, according to the individuals and even for the same individual as per the times of the day, the interpretation of a document varies. However, according to our hypotheses, this difficulty of interpretive ambiguity is absolutely unavoidable. Indeed, any expression is necessarily carrying ambiguities, as expressed by the Spinozist principles (see section 3.2) which affirm that inadequate ideas are inevitable. These ambiguities are, moreover, what makes automatic translation of meaning impossible:

"In Bar-Hillel's demonstration, the elimination of ambiguities in the translation process presupposes the use of 'facts' that are not in the statement to be translated [...] Bar-Hillel argues that these facts are infinite, that it is therefore impossible to completely reduce the ambiguity of natural languages and that it is therefore impossible to achieve a high-level of automatic translation."[69] [AMI 10, p. 48]

We have already approached this question by specifying that the relations created by the symbol between the concrete and the abstract do not have a cardinality "1-1" except in the formal languages which in return neglect the semantic dimension. From then on, it follows a complex game where the symbol will create potentialities of meaning, but with the problem of knowing what meaning that will be:

---

68 The five quotes referenced are all translations of French texts.
69 Translation of French quote.

"Because of the interlocking contexts that define multiple communication situations, there is always another possible meaning. The problem is knowing what the meaning is."[70] [BAL 02, p. 351]

We will see later in section 4.1 how to implement the calculability of meaning through a semantic sphere and a pragmatic solution to this problem.

3.2.11. *The search for the perfect language*

We take the title of this chapter from a book by Umberto Eco [ECO 94b] in which he paints a rich panorama of the different attempts which humans have made to create a language that can reach universality while respecting the constraints of a formal language:

"It is a system of signs:

– between the signs of the system (as long as they are not signs for empty positions) and the question of what is thought (in the widest sense of the word) must exist a bijective relationship: for every object of thought there is one, and only one, sign and *vice versa*;

– signs must be designed in such a way that, wherever an object of thought that can be divided into components is present, the signs of these components are themselves the components of the sign of the object;

– the crucial point, only explicable after the previous requisites: we must invent a system of operating rules for these signs so that, wherever there exists between an object of thought P1 and an object of thought P2 a relationship of consequent reasoning, the P2 sign can be interpreted as a consequence of the P1 sign."[71] [GAU 01, p. 52]

---

70 Translation of French quote.
71 Translation of French quote.

Humans have always tried to transcribe their thoughts into signs so that they can be understood, regardless of place, time or person. To do this, the researchers who tried the experiment faced the same difficulty, namely an attempt to combine two aspects of the language: the content plan and the expression plan.

"A universal language must consider two aspects: a classification of knowledge, which is the work of the philosopher (content plan) and a grammar that organizes the characters in such a way that they refer to things and notions established by this classification (expression plan)."[72] [ECO 94b, p. 264]

However, this difficulty often leads to a theoretical impasse, especially today, where the construction of semantic networks in the form of a hypercomplex graph suggests a detailed control of semantics. However, as Yves Jeanneret remarked:

"The preponderance of this model of graph can induce a theoretical error: that which consists of assimilating the material organization of the expression plan (more exactly the technical part of it) to the process of constructing meaning. The reader is not confronted with computer script."[73] [JEA 07, p. 175]

This theoretical error is often expressed through the lure of believing that the technique is itself able to solve all the problems. Even Gaston Bachelard dreamed that the invention of the radio would provide a technical solution to the communication problems of our society:

"We are on track in the 12th Century, to compose a kind of universal tongue: all languages come to speak, but do not get confused; it is not a tower of Babel; it is, on the contrary, a classification, a very social limitation of all wavelengths, so that everyone can speak without being disturbed [...] in the universal world which is animated by radio, everyone gets along and everyone can listen in peace."[74] [BAC 10, p. 217]

---

72 Translation of French quote.
73 Translation of French quote.
74 Translation of French quote.

It is tempting to dream also of the possibility of this language, allowing pure thought to express itself and thus to settle the conflicts that arise most often from misunderstanding. However, as David Rabouin reminds us, despite all the philosophical attempts and the progress of technology, humans today do not have this pure language:

> "Despite the redoubled efforts of philosophers since Descartes, it does not seem that such a translation into a 'pure' language (language of 'consciousness' or 'concept') is still available to mankind. The language of the phenomenologist (primacy of consciousness) remains entirely crossed by 'aiming', a look that 'revolves around' the thing, 'point of view', 'exteriority' (or 'transcendence' of the object), etc. The language of the logician (primacy of concept) remains entirely supported on what is not just a language of concepts, but a writing, a spatial arrangement of signs on the page on which they are written and which allows them to transcribe 'intuitively' primitive properties like those of order and symmetry, from which it is able to build the fundamental system for its inferences."[75] [RAB 10, p. 38]

A universal language still seems to emerge today. It should not be sought on the side of philosophers, but rather on the side of statisticians who have established a government practice that combines together the moral and quantitative dimensions. As Thomas Berns pointed out, statistics is becoming more and more a universal language that has gradually been established upon the idea of an exhaustive accountancy that would give it a dimension of justice:

> "From this practical point of view, which is above all in a series of techniques related to the keeping of the account book, it is clearly the ideal of an exhaustive accountancy, to which no detail should escape, so that everything remains available. [...] because, as a practical matter, the accounts allow for a representation of the whole as taken from the sum of its parts – a whole thus definitively given since its limits are concretely known – which they can make work for justice."[76] [BER 09b, p. 48]

---

75 Translation of French quote.
76 Translation of French quote.

With the multiplication of open data and the statistical treatments that are linked to them, this justice of numbers and figures tends to become the criterion of truth. It suffices, for example, to show, on television, a graph with a curve that goes up and down so that a minister can argue his point of view and justify his policy[77]. Fortunately, this type of subterfuge has given rise to many remarks and comments, denouncing the lack of seriousness that should be given to such practices. However, it is important to show through this example how it becomes necessary to focus on the double deception of technology and numbers, and how urgent it is becoming to train individuals at this indispensable critical distance that must arise from any interpretation.

3.3. Semantic knowledge management

For a long time presented as a realistic perspective to the development of the Internet, the notion of the Semantic Web has gradually been replaced by that of Linked Open Data. The semantic knowledge management approach that links interoperable data is far more realistic, but it poses very concrete problems, particularly in the application of computer ontologies; problems that Pierre Lévy proposes to solve through a semantic sphere.

3.3.1. *The boundaries of ontologies*

Computer ontologies are enjoying a growing success and are also very controversial due to the limitations of symbolic languages (see section 3.2.9), and as evidenced by the numerous scientific articles devoted to them [GAN 08, FER 09, LIM 10], the advertisements that are made to them, in particular by W3C, and the critics who emanate from their use [RAS 08, ZAC 10a], for example, that the vision of meaning is a little too univocal:

> "The refusal of 'ontologist' computer scientists to consider the multiple dimensions of meaning, condemns them to never be able to properly analyze the uses that are made by their formalisms, therefore, they often remain relatively unuseful."[78] [ZAC 10, p. 187]

---

77 http://owni.fr/2011/01/25/plus-la-delinquance-baisse-plus-la-violence-augmente/
78 Translation of French quote.

There are many definitions of ontology both in the field of computer science and philosophy [VAR 10, NEF 09], for our part, we adopt the generic definition of ontology given by Folch and Habert, because it insists on the central place of the human in the chain of information transmission:

"Ontology is an explicit (formalized) specification of the conceptualization of a domain. As such, it plays a pivotal role between human treatment and the 'mechanical' treatment of information in this domain. It represents the culmination of a process of stabilization, of homologation, through a given community of notions and relations that seem fundamental to it: it is the explanation of a common language. In this sense, ontology is the product of consensus standardization."[79]
[FOL 04, p. 69]

We have only gone over the field of ontologies used to manage knowledge in Web ecosystems; our goal was not to make a complete panorama or a precise analysis, but rather to show their complexity (for a technical explanation, see section 5.1.3.4). Indeed, the design of information on the Web today requires mastering so many parameters that it was necessary to find practical ways to manage this complexity, such as the analogy with knowledge ecosystems.

3.3.2. *The semantic sphere IEML*

For 30 years, Pierre Lévy has been working on collective intelligence and the means of developing it along the three fundamental axes: the semantic axis, more specifically the question of the interoperability of meaning in "digital chaos" [LÉV 11, p. 2], the ethical axis aiming at a better human development through a "knowledge management animated by a free creative conversation" [LÉV 11, p. 4], and the technical axis, whose objective is to automate "as much as possible the symbolic operations that increase cognitive abilities" [LÉV 11, p. 5]. We will only be able to scratch the surface of Pierre Lévy's propositions; a complete thesis would undoubtedly be necessary to present them in detail. In lieu of this, we will instead focus on our understanding of the semantic sphere and the metalanguage of IEML, and present the challenges and what means are being implemented to achieve this.

---

79 Translation of French quote.

3.3.2.1. *Optimizing human symbolic cognition*

The *Groupe de recherché sur la culture et la didactique de l'information*, (French Research Group on the Culture and Didactics of Information or GRCDI) has recently published a report that presents an overview of this group's reflection on informational culture and information didactics [SER 10]. In this report, we find in particular Pascal Duplessis'[80] work on the definition of the issues of information education and the pedagogical objectives associated with these. This very detailed table shows how much educational information is today part of the fundamental building blocks of pedagogy as evidenced by the 12 proposals of the GRCDI for the elaboration of a "documentary information curriculum" and in particular, the fourth proposal, "integrating media education, information literacy and ICT literacy as part of a global information culture" [SER 10].

The IEML program places itself directly within this perspective by attempting to meet the three major challenges of collective intelligence as it pertains to the control of information, and aimed at increasing individual and collective human knowledge, "that of the scientific modeling of symbolic cognition, that of an improvement in the collaborative production of knowledge from the Web data, and finally that of an increase in the autonomous personal capacities used to organize learning and to navigate the flow of information" [LÉV 11, p. 32].

Given the ever-increasing amount of information and the level of complexity that they reach, in particular due to their interconnections, the tools for the symbolic management of information that humanity has put in place are no longer sufficiently effective. They are not adapted for documentary resources which are constantly evolving and which are not only composed of texts but also of sounds, images and videos. Moreover, the symbolic languages of the libraries do not take into account the multiplication of the points of view as is the case with folksonomies. Finally, the symbolic strings that are used to organize the knowledge in libraries are neither interoperable nor computable. This is one of the major issues of the IEML research program.

---

80 http://goo.gl/reA74

To this computability issue, the issue of scientific responsibility is added in the development of these new symbolic technologies. As noted by Olivier Le Deuff in his article on the possibility of a science for collective intelligence, it is probably not necessary to wait until only the commercial businesses develop these technologies whereon they will only have at their disposal tools which we do not control the "ins and outs" of, as is already the case with search engines:

> "The Web and the Internet deserve a more ambitious analysis, otherwise the market spheres will, in effect, soon impose their views towards a deformation economy. P. Levy's project is therefore also to put a little scientific authority in the face of rising popularity mechanisms."[81]

Since what is at stake today, it is effectively a search for a convergence of scientific modeling and the individual organization of knowledge, in order to achieve the collaborative production of knowledge. A challenge that many others, in addition to Pierre Lévy, have been defending already for more than 10 years. Yves Jeanneret expressed this necessity for a methodical work that is undoubtedly ungrateful but nonetheless a producer of knowledge:

> "We cannot be content to look at controversies from a distance, to talk more or less metaphorically about mediation, convention or translation, we have to look closely at them: towards objects, documentary practices, actors, and – I particularly insist on this – the forms of expression. This examination is not a marginal, or secondary, or external aspect of cultural analysis, but a crucial moment. This type of work, methodical and rather ungrateful in principle, produces knowledge."[82]

We owe to the work of Edgar Morin, in particular *Méthode*, the fertile frameworks for thought (see section 3.1.3). However, today we must go further to achieve a profound understanding of social phenomena by providing the research being carried out in the human sciences with more effective tools so as to accurately express concepts and thus calculate "the laws of transformation that govern the transmutation of the different species of symbolic capital" [BOU 01, p. 210].

---

81 goo.gl/tLtMO. Translation of French quote.
82 http://goo.gl/RN4V2. Translation of French quote.

The project of developing a scientific program for collective intelligence is focused fully in this direction. It projects the realization of a "hypercortex" whose purpose is to use the digital storage and computing resources provided by knowledge ecosystems to create a mirror of the symbolic activity that makes it possible to observe it scientifically. Pierre Lévy summarizes the project's ambitions as follows:

> "The Web probably forms a hypertext but it is an opaque hypertext, fragmented between languages, classifications, ontologies and commercial platforms, a hypertext whose nodes are ultimately only physical addresses. If we want to use the Web to coordinate our collective intelligences and share our cultural memories on a new scale; if we want to represent more clearly than today the operations underlying our processes of social cognition, to identify the blind zones of our knowledge and to increase our capacities for critical questioning; if we want to move towards a better cultural understanding and cultivate the efficiency of our creative conversations; if we want to finally increase our capacity to build and interpret digital-based stories using the available computing power, then we need to complete the digital medium with a new addressing layer and semantic computing."[83] [LÉV 11, p. 289]

Many initiatives are already moving in this direction, notably to help national and international multidisciplinary cooperation in order to create structured data and document storage platforms. We are thinking particularly of the initiatives which we have already mentioned in section 5.1.2.5. However, these initiatives offer interoperable data formats, but they do not dispense with notations comprised of alphabetic characters from natural language (often English), which has the major disadvantage of remaining "semantically opaque by construction" [LÉV 11, pp. 197–289].

Indeed, these sequences of characters can always be compared or linked with other character strings, which have the effect of dropping the semantic processing; either in tautology, where the concept is described by a string of characters that describes the concept; or in an endless loop, where the concept is described by a string of characters, itself described by another string of characters and so on. Hence, the need to find a language that frees

---

83 Translation of French quote.

itself from these problems in order to build the semantic sphere necessary for the project of scientific observation of collective intelligence in the sense that:

> "The relationship between the semantic sphere and the hypercortex is therefore a relationship between a scientific instrument of observation (the hypercortex) and the projection system that organizes it (the semantic sphere)."[84] [LÉV 11, p. 176]

3.3.2.2. Addressing concepts in a semantic sphere

We all know how much the methodological aspect guarantees scientific coherence, particularly in the hyper-complex research that concerns knowledge ecosystems; and how computer languages make it possible to express this coherence, provided that a unique relationship between a symbolic form (string of characters) and a concept is respected. What Pierre Lévy proposes with the semantic sphere IEML is precisely to be able to answer this methodological necessity of the mathematical formalization of the concepts allowing for unique and calculable addressing in "a system of mathematical-linguistic coordinates serving as reference" [LÉV 11, p. 225].

At this point, it is important to emphasize that the goal of IEML is neither to create a machine capable of calculating meaning in the manner of humans nor to see collective intelligence as the means to a simulation of all the knowledge needed to apprehend all contexts, which proves to be an impossible task, as expressed by Jean-Pierre Balpe following on his experiences of the automatic generation of texts:

> "To obtain a programming of meaning as effective as that carried out by the human brain, a program is needed which has human characteristics, that is, constantly capturing information, and capable of constantly reconfiguring its representations. In this case, unless it is a collective intelligence, that is, not to neglect any information being issued anywhere and anytime, this programming will also have the human defects of non-exhaustiveness and non-homogeneity: it will not allow a

---

84 Translation of French quote.

semantic mastery of everything on everything and will include specialized zones."[85] [BAL 02, p. 349]

Conceived as "a useful scientific convention", the semantic sphere IEML is a network of concepts related to each other following inclusion, intersection and union operations whose coordinates are addressable with the IEML metalanguage.

"Any establishment of meaning is based on a weaving of effective relationships in a set of possible relationships: the meaning is a setting in context, a networking of information, meanings and knowledge." [BAL 02, p. 345]

To arrive at this effective weaving of the relations of meaning, Pierre Lévy insisted on the double condition to respect and to know that this language:

– first, is "a regular ideographic language" [LÉV 11, p. 237] which allows, by its regular grammar, an arithmetic and logical calculability, and is ideographic to encode meaning and not sounds;

– second, there is an "isomorphism between textual objects and semantic topology" in order to be able to perform the same cognitive manipulations with IEML as a natural language.

To meet these two conditions, IEML is based on an analysis of the "general structure of cognitive operations on linguistic objects" [LÉV 11, p. 238] to propose a language made of textual units consisting of:

– six layers: primitive, event, relation, idea, sentence and text;

– three classes: verbs, nouns and auxiliaries;

– three roles: substance, attribute and mode.

Each of these textual units and their relations is being expressed by numbers. Therefore, we can break the knot for the problem of the calculability of meaning, the diagnosis of which Descartes expressed already:

---

85 Translation of French quote.

"Descartes realizes that the crux of the question is [...] If someone were able to quantify all the simple ideas from which all the ideas that we are capable of thinking are then engendered, and assigned to each a character, we could later articulate this kind of mathematics of thinking, just as we do for numbers – whereupon the words of our languages would refer to confusing ideas."[86] [ECO 94b, p. 250]

The IEML metalanguage will allow us to formally describe a semantic circuit which represents the meaning that a document expresses in a natural language, in a photo, a sound and an architecture. The transition from this "natural" sense to the "formal" sense corresponds to a linguistic function that Pierre Lévy calls "a semantic inference" [LÉV 11, p. 236 and 265] and which it breaks down:

– in the construction rules of syntagmatic circuits: the grammar of relations between textual units;

– in the construction rules of paradigmatic circuits corresponding to the semantic relationships that link these textual units: etymological, taxonomic, symmetrical, serial, etc.

By coding, in a dictionary, the rules that correspond to the axioms of the IEML theory and their equivalent in natural language, it becomes possible to translate an IEML text into a semantic circuit and its natural language equivalent. In summary:

"In the model of the mind that adopts the semantic sphere as a coordinate system, an idea is represented by a unit of semantic information [...]. The concept is coded by a USL [...] which is automatically converted into a circuit of the semantic sphere and translated into natural languages. The affect is coded by a semantic current (polarity, intensity) flowing in this circuit. Finally, the percept [...] is addressed by a URL."[87] [LÉV 11, p. 270]

---

86 Translation of French quote.
87 Translation of French quote.

Finally, we can translate the model of the IEML mind in the diagram (Figure 3.4) to show how the affect of an individual will be able to be modeled by the activation of a semantic current between a potentiality of precepts and a potentiality of concepts. Each address of the semantic sphere is defined by a USL (Uniform Semantic Locator) which corresponds to a particular node in the topological network. This node can be connected with other nodes according to two main types of links: paradigmatic and syntagmatic. We find here our symbolic bipartition between the order of the abstract and the concept (paradigm) and the order of the concrete and the form (syntagma).

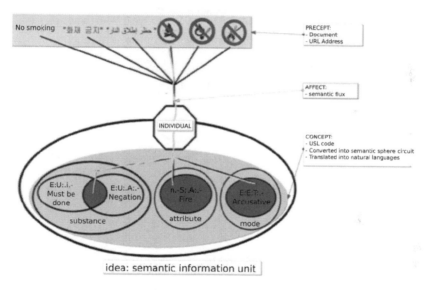

Figure 3.4. *IEML idea diagram. For a color version of the figure, see www.iste.co.uk/szoniecky/ecosystems.zip*

From a syntagmatic point of view, the nodes are linked by their degree of complexity to the statement ranging from the speech to the morpheme by way of the sentence, the words and the morphemes. From the paradigmatic point of view, the connections between nodes are:

– etymological: this connection connects concepts with the more basic concepts that compose them. For example, the concept of anthropology is composed of the concepts of *anthropos* (human being) and *logos* (speech, study and rhetoric);

– taxonomic: in the sense that one concept is a subset of another, e.g. philosophy and mathematics maintain a taxonomic connection within the concept of organized knowledge;

– symmetrical: the related concepts thus indicate a complementarity in a field, e.g. the different colors or the connection between the guardian and the prisoner;

– serial: this connection is the result of a storage of concepts following a linear gradient. Pierre Lévy uses a double gradient "more abstract/more concrete" to build the matrices of concepts; however, we can conceive of others. For example, a gradient from the most democratic to the least democratic in relation to which the following concepts would find a place: absolutism, aristocracy, autocracy, despotism, fascism, monarchy and totalitarianism.

Along with the semantic sphere and the IEML metalanguage, we have tools that offer the ability to automate conceptual writing by inventing particular views of the semantic sphere. For example, to develop collaborative systems used for interpreting an event using the same conceptual referential or to create conceptual matrices which, like Mendeleyev's periodic table of elements, "one of the earlier beautiful visualizations of complex data" [STE 10, p.4], classify and generate ideas; or develop survey tools for knowledge ecosystems [HAC 12].

> "Instead of requiring expression writing one after the other, IEML is designed from the outset to allow the programming of write functions, that is, the automatic generation of IEML expression functions. This property can be used, for example, in digital storytelling, metaprogramming of game scenarios or interactive simulation design."[88] [LÉV 11, p. 93]

This very succinct presentation of the semantic sphere and metalanguage IEML aims to show the key principles of the scientific research program on collective intelligence proposed by Pierre Lévy. For a more detailed approach, we invite readers to consult the books of Pierre Lévy, including [LÉV 11] and articles where we present our contributions to this exciting project, for which there is still much to do.

---

88 Translation of French quote.

In this chapter, we wanted to show how the modeling principles we propose come from a process of maturation that has evolved a simple analogy between the work on knowledge and that of gardening towards a preliminary graphic design, next the development of prototypes, and finally generic principles of modeling.

Building on these foundations, we continued our work of cultivating the analogy of the garden to build a platform for the development of knowledge ecosystems (see Chapter 5: Web Platform Specifications for Knowledge Ecosystems) which we have field tested in several research projects. However, before presenting these works, let us first examine the graphic specifications for the modeling of informational existences in the following chapter.

4

Graphical Specifications for Modeling Existences

This new approach
leads to thinking of each visual culture
as an ecosystem composed of
a multitude of imaging systems[1].
Bernard Darras

But because the similitudes that form the graphics of the world
are one "cog" out of alignment with those that form its discourse, knowledge
and the infinite labor it involves
find here the space that is proper to them:
it is their task to weave their way across this distance,
pursuing an endless zigzag course
from resemblance to what resembles it.
Michel Foucault[2]

In Chapter 3, we presented the principles for modeling knowledge ecosystems. In this chapter, we would like to emphasize the representation of these models by showing that they must be designed as diagrams. More precisely, the models that we design are the visual representations of an existence produced in order to understand this said existence and to potentially deduce new properties from it. The objective of modeling is to

1 Translation of French quote.
2 Translation of quote from https://archive.org/stream/FoucaultMichelTheOrderOfThingsAn
ArchaeologyOfTheHumanSciences/Foucault,%20Michel%20-%20The%20Order%20of%20
Things%20-%20An%20Archaeology%20of%20the%20Human%20Sciences_djvu.txt.

represent in a simple way the processes of signification by placing human interpretation, at the heart of the representation, into a composition involving knowledge-existences in an interactive information design.

After state-of-the-art graphical modeling systems, the aim of this chapter is to specify the diagrammatic rules that will be applied to graphically model informational existences and their relations in a knowledge ecosystem.

4.1. Principles of graphical modeling

In order to better understand the ins and outs of a project and to communicate them as efficiently as possible, the transition to graphical modeling becomes unavoidable. This chapter will present two examples of a graphical modeling system in complete opposition to both the principles and the graphs, in order to define the boundaries of a state-of-the-art system without having to overmultiply the examples. We start with a presentation of Unified Modeling Language (UML) that offers generic graphical rules for the modeling of projects. This language illustrates how a graphical representative system can become a standardized language for modeling and, more generally, for project management. Next, we discuss new ways of representing musical partitions to show how they offer interesting perspectives for design. The end of this chapter will emphasize the important graphic principles, firstly as they pertain to dynamism and interactivity, as well as the relations between inside and outside relationships.

4.1.1. *Unified modeling language*

To facilitate the work of IT developers, engineers have created modeling languages to capture needs, analyze them and design appropriate solutions. The UML initiative appeared in the 1990s with the goal of unifying several modeling languages and thereby facilitating communications between large industrial groups such as IBM, Microsoft, Oracle, DEC, HP, Rational, Unisys, etc.

Today, UML has become a standard modeling language whose very detailed specifications are accessible to anyone and everyone[3]. UML offers a series of 13 graphics, which are organized into two major sets: structure and

---

3 Link to the official site of UML: http://www.omg.org/spec/UML/

behavior[4]. UML provides a graphical grammar to describe the design and development stages. This language makes it possible to multiply the axes of description of a project by showing, according to the use cases, the necessary information to understand and discuss the steps of conception and realization. Here is an example for the organization of these diagrams as proposed by Laurent Audibert[5]:

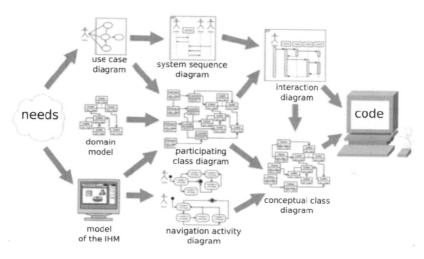

Figure 4.1. *Organization of UML diagrams*

From the perspective of modeling knowledge ecosystems, UML could provide the graphical elements and diagram models required, since it uses a common vocabulary such as: actors, documents, concepts, etc. However, one of the basic principles of this language is in complete contradiction to the ecosystem approach. Indeed for UML, the actors are external to the system and are considered only within an interactive dialogue approach and as such are not explicitly involved. It can be understood that UML defends this principle of the external actor as part of an approach that aims to model a computer system; however, in an approach that aims at modeling knowledge, we are not able to externalize the actor, who for us, is at the heart of the relations between interiority and externality.

---

4 For a detailed description of the different types of graphics UML, see http://laurent-audibert.developpez.com/Cours-UML/
5 Illustration: http://laurent-audibert.developpez.com/Cours-UML

Similarly, concerning the conceptual dimension which, according to our principles of modeling, has a fundamental place in equal proportion to the other three, according to UML principles, it has no particular existence, but rather infuses each graphical element with a textual form. Another point of divergence between UML and our modeling principles concerns the possible multiplication of viewpoints. After the work of collective modeling and the development of the UML graphic, the latter needs to be as explicit as possible and must not leave any room for ambiguity or controversy. Conversely, within knowledge ecosystems, controversy should not be eliminated, but rather, on the contrary, be perfectly visible since it is from this that scientific work originates.

Despite these drawbacks regarding the modeling principles, we consider UML as a concrete example of what we want to achieve with our generic knowledge ecosystem modeling project. It seems, to us, important to take inspiration from this language, in terms of its simplicity and standardization in terms of adapting it to interactions and interoperability in the human sciences, and in particular the digital humanities.

4.1.2. *Graphic partitions and diagrams*[6]

In contrast to UML's graphic principles, musical notation shows how an intellectual technology graphically organizes the collective intelligence of a human group seeking ways to express harmony in a defined spacetime. In the history of musical notation, since the 1950s, we have observed an evolution of classical notation processes, which tends towards the use of diagrams possessing an informational existence which is reminiscent of a change in a conceptual model, from a modernist vision towards an ecosystem approach [LAT 12].

Classical musical scores provide musicians with direction on what to play when, and how. These behave like performers who obey to the letter of the sequence of the score; they are one of the many links in the process, and they can be replaced by another musician with equal technical skills. We find here the ancient definition of the symbolic contract between an artifact and its meaning [DEC 03] which remains valid independent of the person. Therefore, the sign on the musical score that signifies "C", by collective agreement, will be interpreted as "C" regardless of who will read the score.

---

6 This chapter lists the work carried out in collaboration with Lenka Strenka [LEN 14].

There is no equivocation between the sign and the meaning associated with it, just as it is within a computer language where the signs are linked to one and only one function.

If classical scores are effective for recording, archiving, disseminating, learning and building a social relationship for music, they are hence subject to the intrinsic limits of symbolic languages as the illusion of a complete fit between form and meaning [RAB 10, p.62] and the limitation of knowledge by auto-referencing (see section 3.2.9). In order to overcome these limits and to invent other forms of music, creators like M. Feldman have experimented with the use of the diagrams that J.-Y. Bosseur described as follows:

> "Notation is only really graphical to the extent that the composer departs from the symbolic signs traditionally used for the notation of durations and establishes a principle of analogy between the time and the corresponding spatial measure."[7] [BOS 14]

In order to create a score, the composer's task is to recognize the generative power of the gesture, to identify the operation that the gesture has in the graph and the outline it generates. When it comes to a diagram (and not a plan or schema), the inscribed gesture shows more than the eye perceives [JED 07]. Therefore, we cannot find in a diagram a demonstration, a simplification or a flow diagram; nevertheless, we discover a mode of operation which puts into operation the diagrammatic machinery which in turn generates a meaning.

The graphic partition in terms of diagram interfaces between the real and the virtual shows a potentiality of gestures in the actuality of the dynamics of the graphics. Unlike computer languages and schemas like UML, which set strict boundaries for the interpretation of signs by forcing the relationship between the physical and conceptual dimensions in the manner of a *topos*, diagrams follow *chora* principles [BER 09a, pp. 30–35; ZAM 03, p. 22; BOU 11, p. 80] which, in the form of a screen [DEL 88, p. 103] represents information, and at the same time generates the events that produce them. This type of partition, and more generally the diagrams, associate reading and writing to create a potentiality of gestures by playing on the analogies between the form and the meaning, and not on the register of similarity for

---

7 Translation of French quote.

the one and the other, but instead follow a reciprocal modulation [BAT 05, p. 13]. Rather than highlighting the univocity of the relationship between a sign and a meaning as schemas do, the graphical analogy of diagrams multiplies the relationships between exteriority and interiority in the manner of analogist ontology (see section 3.2.6 for more on the ontological principles of Descola).

A diagram designed in this way has its own existence, which is related to a living existence by these internal dynamisms and the potentiality of interaction that it induces within the context of its perception. We can refer to a synergy that makes the diagram the guide for the realization of a dynamic process always being developed, like a work in progress. Due to the dynamism of the diagram, the potentialities of relationships unfold and develop an ecosystem of information and communication.

By going beyond the idea of fixing in the sign the matter of meaning, as with the classical score or computer languages, we develop the dynamics necessary for instantaneous intuitions. However, this vital aspect of information ecosystems, as it pertains to the analogies and diagrams representing them, does not exclude the question regarding the viability of communications at which computer languages are particularly effective.

As a diagram, graphic scores show what is inaccessible to immediate perception. They are aimed at an objective that is not explicitly presented but which remains to be realized. The strict obedience imposed by computer languages directs informational practice towards the performance and the mechanical efficiency of the performers. To explore other types of practices and knowledge, the journey via diagrams opens up the perspectives of information ecosystems where the relationship between form and meaning can be multiplied by an infinite number of viewpoints. What matters is the emergence of a "weaving of knowledge" from the interrelationship of experience of each one through the intermediary of a diagram.

4.1.3. *Fixed image versus dynamic diagram*

Among the essential references concerning the graphic representation of knowledge, it is necessary to quote the theoretical point of view of Jacques Bertin [BER 99] and the language of R statistics from the point of view of technologies. However, beyond the quality and importance of these two approaches from the point of view of data design [REY 17], they pose a problem in their relationship to the interactivity and dynamism of representations. Our approach to the graphic modeling of ecosystems necessarily involves representations capable of evolving both by interaction with human users, and also in the relationships that these representations maintain with each other.

In his graphical semiology, Bertin defined the "representation" with explicit and strict starting constraints, notably on the fact that it must be designed as a graph "which is representable or printable [...] on a sheet of white paper" [BER 99, p. 42]. These initial constraints are quite understandable in a world where paper remains the essential means of communication, although in terms of the World Wide Web, they appear counterproductive. Think of Hans Rosling whose work on the representation of data emphasizes the dynamism of representations and the importance of organizing this dynamism within a coherent narrative.

Conversely, the diagram, as support for information and reasoning [THI 06, p. 8], is defined by Noëlle Batt according to an analogous and living dimension that confirms our ecosystem vision of modeling:

> "The diagram is also the appropriate time for Bachelardian reverie which authorizes the implementation of analogy, which does not exclude the possibility that it takes forms that are a little bit crude, perhaps sometimes a little primary, allowing for this the same supports, slightly orthodox connections (like a portion of primordial soup where very remote things *a priori* can associate and cultivate) and which allows for progress in the thought to be made, even if this progression follows an erratic or turbulent trajectory [...] The thinking is done by diagramming."[8] [BAT 05, p. 22]

The ever-growing presence on the Web of dynamic graphics as well as the possibilities offered by "generative design" for interactivity with humans and graphic components makes it necessary to interconnect the skills of knowledge technologies and graphic designers [LAV 09, HUT 00]:

---

8 Translation of French quote.

"The constant flow of dynamic content in modern media and the easy access to vast compilations of data have allowed the emergence of generative design, but have come at the cost of freehand layouts and illustrations. Given the amount of content we have to deal with today, this translates into a greater necessity than progress. However, we are convinced that this new way of working is opening new perspectives, and it is also imposing new requirements on graphic designers."[9] [KLA 09, p. 225]

This rapprochement between intellectual technologies and dynamic graphics is also linked to an equally important challenge, that of the "correspondence between semantic 'proximity' and onscreen proximity or 'interactive' proximity" [MEL 06, p. 38]. It is precisely towards this last point that diagrammatic conceptions can help us. Indeed, as Franck Jedrzejewski remarked in his thesis:

"The diagram combines in a thousand forms an intelligible series that the human gesture organizes using its own resources, suggesting that the tool in which the territory metamorphoses gives it meaning. The meaning brought about through the unveiling of the gesture claims the path that created it. The outcome of meaning is at this price: reconstructing the gesture in the diagram to understand how the subject contrives the meaning."[10] [JED 07, p. 17]

We have insisted on the importance of modeling the knowledge being made; let us take note now of how through the dynamic and interactive graphics that are the diagrams, modeling makes a transition between the gesture being made and the knowledge that it leads to. In this perspective, we must extend the field of hypertext by introducing gestures that, in addition to texts, sounds and images, enrich knowledge ecosystems. Therefore, as a result of the diagram, it becomes possible to build a representation whose objective will be to show the dynamisms of a knowledge being made using the ecosystem modeling principles:

---

9 Translation of French quote.
10 Translation of French quote.

"The diagram has the function of representing, clarifying and explaining something that is related to the relationship between the part and the whole and between each of the parts to the other (whether this is a natural whole like a flower or a mathematical, algebraic or geometric set), but it can also express a dynamic journey, an evolution, the result of the same phenomenon."[11] [BAT 05, p. 7]

4.2. Semantic maps

Faced with the challenges for the formalization of interpretations and the user-friendliness of human–machine interfaces [ILL 75], map interfaces offer the advantage of rendering the formalization of work transparent by giving users more freedom with which to express their intuitions at different levels of scale, while providing a "mirror" that reflects collective or individual intellectual practices [ROS 13].

"It's not just a question of linking a macro scale to a plunge into micro details, but also of identifying the processes by which the implementation of actors and arguments move, changing frameworks and modalities by producing effects remote to their context of appearance."[12] [CHA 15, section 5]

We propose analyzing the principles of cartographic interfaces according to three complementary aspects: space, time and concepts. We want to show how these principles form the basis for designing generic and user-friendly maps to produce and generate interpretations.

4.2.1. *Maps of physical spaces*

Geographical mapping is probably one of the oldest attempts to graphically organize physical spaces so as to describe them and guide users in their explorations. The major progress of this system of information organization lies in the adoption of a common repository which allowed for the harmonizing of viewpoints and for the transfer from a purely subjective vision, like the portolan chart, to an entire science of cartography. It should

---

11 Translation of French quote.
12 Translation of French quote.

be noted, however, that although geographical coordinates are now fully interoperable as a consequence of GPS technologies and advances in online mapping tools, subjectivity problems still persist. Jean-Christophe Victor demonstrated this clearly in his program "Beneath Maps" (*Le dessous des cartes*) dedicated to the fluctuations of borders according to the country where the maps are being consulted. Nevertheless, it is today very important to have at your disposal extremely simple tools to convert a click on an image into geographical coordinates. This is one of the most effective ergonomic principles for formalizing very precise data by way of a very simple gesture. Similarly, the change of scale (+ zoom, - zoom) and the movement of the image are ergonomic principles particularly useful for navigating information and selecting a fragment.

Figure 4.2. *Gallica map tools*

This is also what the *Bibliothèque nationale de France* or BNF (National Library of France) posted on the Gallica platform, a scanned document that can be navigated, where the user has at his disposal a set of tools that act as a vocabulary of cartographic interfaces, such as the mini-map, rotation function, content selection and coordinate sharing (Figure 4.2). This latest tool is perhaps one of the most interesting from Gallica, since it makes it possible to consider a very precise and interoperable analysis of scanned documents by providing a specific reference point of a scanned document fragment. With this tool, we can use a reference as a resource annotation that would aim to develop a pitch or question the meaning of the fragment. For example, in the fragment below[13]: what do the balls in the tree in the frontispieces of a 16th Century work represent?

Figure 4.3. *Example of a Gallica fragment*

4.2.2. *Time maps*

In the digital ecosystem, the precise expression of temporality is extremely simple since computer events, such as the click, automatically generate a reference for a precise and instantaneous execution in the order of a millisecond. It is therefore very easy to compile these events in order to trace the temporality of usage and to, above all, synchronize them at the global scale. This global synchronization of time is one of the main consequences to the digitization of the planet. If the gain in terms of the interoperability of information is huge, we must not overlook the dangers of this trend "whose issues are analyzed through an 'allegory of the anthill' extrapolating the trend of hyper synchronization being implemented by networks" [STI 04, p. 14].

This hyper synchronization unfolds mainly through the perspective of "real time" and a "liquid" society [BAU 06] where information flows continuously and accumulates traces without having time to interpret them. This phenomenon encourages us to react without thinking, such as the ant driven by pheromones or the billiard ball that bounces. In the face of this urgency in immediacy, the challenge of temporal mapping is to provide

13 Link to the perennial Resource:
http://gallica.bnf.fr/iiif/ark:/12148/bpt6k311658q/f7/1211.5837875467491,1415.3365147170
991,1182.156777342453,717.9765738096819/7090,4300/0/native.jpg

consistency to the flow of information in order to show or express historical dynamics and to create the conditions for reflexivity and argumentation. The representation of these historical consistencies is a good way to respond to the need for reflexivity, as they offer support for interpretation.

Figure 4.4. *Dendrochronology*

There are natural models of historical representation, such as dendrochronology or stratigraphy, but many other models [ROS 13] exist, even if the most used is that of the horizontal frieze. It simultaneously makes visible the precise dates, periods and synchronization of different themes. The digital versions of these friezes also use cartographic systems to simultaneously navigate through time by changing scale, and to define very precisely a date or a period. Digital technology also offers the great advantage of animating representations so as to show more explicitly historical dynamics, as Hans Rosling demonstrates in his lecture on the evolution of human development.

Figure 4.5. *Stratigraphy*

4.2.3. *Maps of conceptual spaces*

The idea of representing concepts and organizing them in the form of an image or a drawing is not a recent one, and it was being used by Raymond Lulle as early as the 13th century.

Today, conceptual cartography has become far more abstract and favors representations in the form of networks, where the positions of concepts are calculated by algorithms that optimize the placement of nodes for better visibility or according to thematic weightings [QUE 13]. Here again, these digital representations are adapted to cartographic uses such as zoom, displacement and selection, which, by multiplying the display parameters, makes it possible to express a particular point of view (compare the figures below). However, the complexity of algorithm representations makes the coordinate system used to position the elements opaque. The "computational reason" [PAR 16] then takes precedence over our ability to discern the arguments, which leads us to sterile controversies that are all the more prominent the more the data used to construct the representations are not accessible.

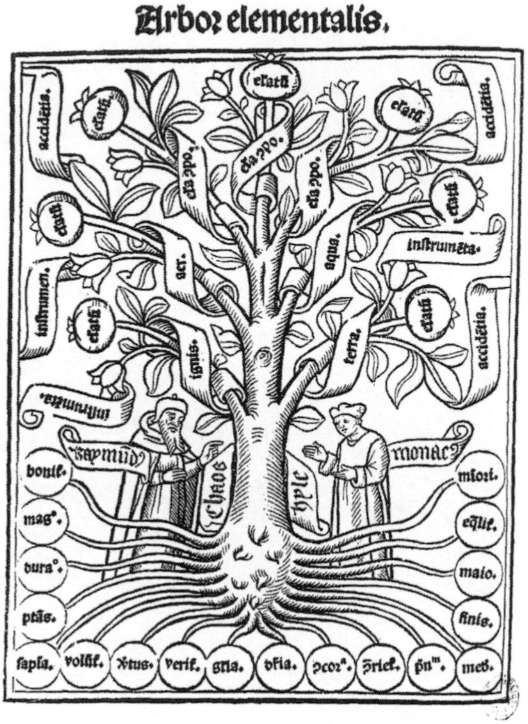

Arbor elementalis.

Figure 4.6. *Tree of elements*

Making coordinate systems understandable and giving users control over positioning is more in line with the researcher's job, to express these intuitions in the form of understandable arguments being put forward by a community. In this perspective, the cartographic principle of choosing a coordinate by simply clicking on a basemap can be used to add a semantic dimension to this click. Depending on the coordinate system used by the basemap, the program will give the click a particular semantic value. Potentially, any image develops a graphic semiology [REY 17] that gives it its meaning. However, in order to make a semantic coordinate system explicit, the graphical semiotics used must in turn be sufficiently explicit.

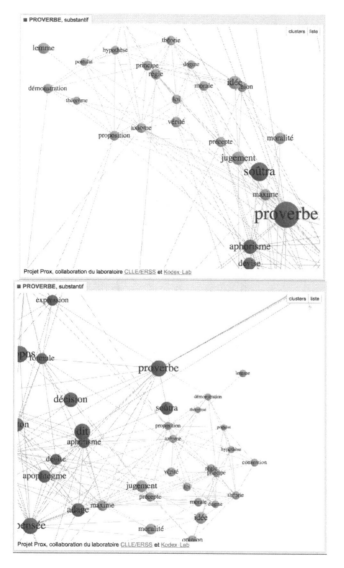

Figure 4.7. *Proxemics of the word "proverb"[14]. For a color version of the figure, see www.iste.co.uk/szoniecky/ecosystems.zip*

The simplest form of graphic semiology that can be considered as a coordinate system is that of a circle which defines a boundary between what belongs to a conceptual field and what is foreign to it. A click inside the

14 Searchable network here: http://www.cnrtl.fr/proxemie/proverbe

circle means that it belongs to this conceptual field, and a click outside the circle means that it does not belong to this conceptual field. By adding another circle, the coordinate system is transformed into a Venn diagram (see section 2.3.2), which makes it possible to represent the logical interactions between two conceptual spaces (Figure 4.8). It is thus possible to multiply the circles and their interactions; however, the diagram quickly becomes overly complex, in turn making it difficult for users to control semantic coherence (Figure 4.9).

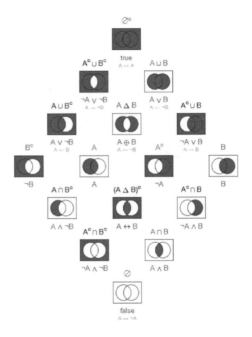

Figure 4.8. *Venn logic. For a color version of the figure, see www.iste.co.uk/szoniecky/ecosystems.zip*

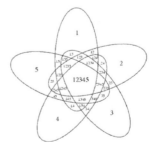

Figure 4.9. *Venn diagram with five entries*

Another graphically simple coordinate system is the axis where one end defines the minimum and the other the maximum. To express semantic coordinates, we associate an end of the axis with a concept, so that the user selects a point and defines its position relative to the concept. In this case, the expression of the user will be more or less weighted according to its proximity to the end. For example, through the position of the vertical red line in Figure 4.10, the user expresses his point of view more by the choice (or not) of a concept than a binary way, which in turn makes it possible to quantify this interpretation so as to compare it with others.

Figure 4.10. *Conceptual axis*

As a result of the scaling tool proposed by D3.js, a JavaScript library for information design (see section 5.2.4.2.2), you can transfer a position on a web page to another value that will at the same time be easier to use for the calculation of, for example, a percentage, and more graphically explicit, for example, a color. Figure 4.10 shows how the selection of a point on the axis expresses both a percentage value (71%) and the color of the concept on a color scale ranging from darkest to brightest. The percentage scale has a "0% → 100%" range in order to be able to signify:

– "0%": the concept has no "power to act", it is invisible and has no influence over the event;

– "100%": the concept is at its maximum "power to act", it is extremely bright, its influence is at maximum, and as such it "illuminates" the event.

In order to express a complex interpretation in which the elements maintain a relation that is both complementary and antagonistic, a concept is added to the axis origin (Figure 4.11). By becoming bidirectional, the conceptual axis gives the user the opportunity to choose the scope of the conceptual field that corresponds to his interpretation, for example, in order to categorize the importance of "good" and "bad" for a particular event. We can use this type of axis to accentuate the opposition between two concepts as per the figure, wherein the concept on the right is the antonym to the concept on the left. However, the concepts can also be complementary as shown in Figure 4.12, which makes it possible to evaluate the adequacy of both the literal sense and the literal meaning in relation to a proverb.

Figure 4.11. *Bidirectional conceptual axis*

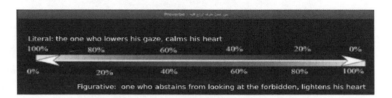

Figure 4.12. *Complementary conceptual axis*

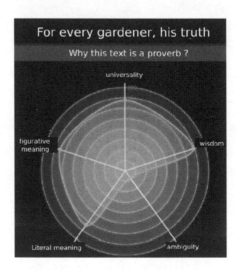

Figure 4.13. *Conceptual radar*

For an expression that is a little more complex, we can multiply the conceptual axes and represent them in the form of radar. The expression of a user will then correspond to a surface that in turn can be compared with other expressions in order to deduce common areas signifying a consensus, those that are empty are *a priori* unimportant, or those populated by a single user and which are the index of a polemic.

Another semantic mapping method based on a conceptual axis consists of crossing two right-angle axes in order to define a reference that gives the rules for transcribing a graphic expression (point, line and plane) into semantic coordinates. There are many examples of this type of semantic mapping, such as the taxonomy of ideas proposed by David McCandless. From these static graphs, we can add a semantic layer in order to make dynamic the arguments they present, and elicit the controversies through the simple displacement or modification of the original graphic expression. For example, we used the idea of taxonomy to conceptually map an event through the automatic generation of tweets with the semantic coordinates defined by the marker (see section 2.3.3). In another example, a click on the wheel of emotions (Figure 5.15) creates an expression from EmotionML[15], the emotion modeling language, by referring to a particular emotion in the ontology of emotions [BER 13], for example, fear: *purl.obolibrary.org/obo/MFOEM_000026*. Stored in a database, this information can then be used to populate a search engine, infer statistics or build dynamic and interactive diagrams that can be used to navigate the corpus.

We could multiply the examples of conceptual cartography as they proliferate. The dynamic semantization of these graphics to make them both interoperable and interactive promises to be one of the major challenges for knowledge engineering, E-education and collective intelligence, that nevertheless finds in this immense project, a common perspective for development.

4.2.4. *Interpretation maps*

We define interpretation as the linking of physical spaces with conceptual spaces by an actor located in the "here and now". To physical spaces, to times and to conceptual spaces, two dimensions must be added in order to successfully map interpretations: the actors and the relations.

Presently, the mapping of the actors occupies a preponderant place in the digital ecosystem, as evidenced by the "big five of the Web" (GAFAM) whose importance is quantified by the number of actors that compose them,

15 Link to the specification of this language: https://www.w3.org/TR/emotionml/

and who are potentially consumers, and thus it is necessary to target "purchasing power" and above all capture attention [CIT 14]. In order to do this, the digital devices used by GAFAM minimize the potential for interpretation ("I like" or "+") to confiscate the discernment power of individuals who no longer master the consequences of their choices. In contrast to these practices, we wish to contribute to the development of the interpretative society that Yves Citton is appealing for:

> "I would like to suggest that our 'knowledge societies' deserve to be analyzed as primarily cultures of interpretation – and that bringing interpretive issues back to the fore should lead us to a profound review of our vision of social interactions, our mapping of knowledge, the structuring of our higher education institutions and the formulation of our political demands."[16] [CIT 10, p. 8]

To carry out this project, we design interpretation mapping systems that aim to represent the discernment power of individuals in the form of a "swarm of small inclinations". Figure 4.14 shows how to organize these small inclinations by displaying the relations that an actor will instantiate between the document layers corresponding to the physical spaces and semantic maps representing physical spaces.

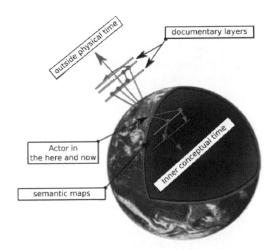

Figure 4.14 *Spatio-temporal mapping of interpretations*

---

16 Translation of French quote.

The first aspect that seems important to us is that of the dynamics between the external-physical and the inner-conceptual dimensions. In terms of representation, the sphere is an adequate shape to demonstrate this opposition and above all define fractal scales according to whether we consider the sphere of the local and individual point of view with the bubble [SLO 02], the macro sphere with the globe [SLO 11] or the collective sphere with the *ecume* [SLO 06]. The surface of this sphere represents the boundary between the inside and the outside. Its thickness is variable according to the number of actors occupying its surface. A thin membrane for the bubble, a thick crust for the globe and the "foam" interface of the *ecume*.

The temporality peculiar to existences in an ecosystem can be conceived as a pulsation between the exterior and the interior. In terms of representation, this pulsation can take the form of a point which, after a fixed or irregular interval, appears and disappears. We can also represent this pulsation by a line that oscillates between several spatial points like the gestures of a conductor beating the measure. Such a representation has the advantage of offering a rich graphical vocabulary that corresponds well with our existence modeling diagram (see section 4.3.3). The spatial points connected by the conductor's gesture correspond to the end of an outer-physical branch on the one side and to the end of an interior-conceptual root, on the other side: the beat of the pulse is equivalent to the instantiation by an actor to the relations between these points. This representation makes possible a pulsation composed of several points, which can be marked in the physical and conceptual dimensions according to the positions of the actor in the physical hierarchy or in the conceptual network. Such a model allows us to represent the different temporalities of this existential pulsation (Figure 4.14).

With each expression of a relationship between the physical and conceptual planes, the user creates the existential pulsation of an actor. These pulsations build the representation of the existence of the actor within the knowledge ecosystem. In the words of Leibniz quoted by Deleuze, we record with this device "small perceptions" and "small inclinations" by which to model the "fabric of the soul" of the actors [DEL 03].

The impact of the digital on the usage of knowledge leads to new temporal paradigms which, while accentuating the control of time and space through techniques and policies, also give individuals the means to develop and share their inner lives. Our ambition is to design and develop digital tools allowing this culture of interiority by exploring the physical traces that humanity has left throughout the course of its history.

4.3. Graphical modeling rules

With our theoretical frameworks in place, let us now define which graphical modeling rules we can use. These rules must be simple so as to facilitate their use. In order to define this simplicity, we will propose an easy-to-understand analogy for when we evaluate it, as Emmanuel Sander proposes, in relation to the "number of levels of abstraction necessary to find a relevant property" [SAN 00, p. 190]. The analogy with which we have been working with for some time is that of the garden (see section 2.3.2). Let us examine how to formalize this analogy with respect to the theoretical principles (see Chapter 4) and graphics that we have defined.

The graphic principles which we use are very simple. They are based on the use of four geographical shapes (rectangle, hexagon, circle and line), each representing one of the existential dimensions of the model (physical, actor, concept and relation). Unlike representations built with tools like GEPHI, which shape a single network of nodes and links, our graphical modeling principles involve four overlapping networks that do not denature the existential dimension and the specific characteristics of each of these networks.

4.3.1. *Physical dimensions*

The physical dimensions correspond to the "extensive parts" discussed by Spinoza and the "physicalities" by Descola. They are the physical dimensions of existence, for instance, a library, a bookshelf, a book, its cover, its pages, the ink of the text, etc. They are subject to fundamental physical laws and can therefore be measured, weighed and broken down into fragments. They are represented by rectangles with a title and correspond to the branches of a plant. These rectangles can be seen as nested and can be used to define a tree of parts.

Figure 4.15. *Modeling physical dimensions*

4.3.2. *Actors*

The actors are the entities responsible for the creation of the relations within a given space and time; they are represented by hexagons with a title. In the analogy with the garden, the actors correspond to seeds. They too can interweave, for example, to signify that a particular person belongs to a particular institution. Actors belonging to several institutions will be able to place themselves at the intersection of these institutions in the manner of a Venn diagram, unlike physical dimensions which cannot be part of two sets simultaneously. For example, in the representation below, "Actor 2" belongs to both "Institution 1" and "Institution 2". A circle is associated with the actor to signify its interiority; it is within this circle that the concepts related to each actor occur.

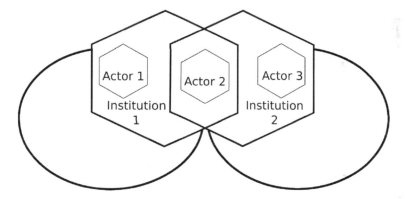

Figure 4.16. *Modeling actors*

4.3.3. *Concepts*

Concepts correspond to the semantic dimensions of modeling, either in the form of a key word or even in the form of a sentence. It is important to note that a word in a physical dimension does not correspond to a concept whose meaning is not reducible to a representation, and as such must continually renegotiate with its self and with others. It thus follows that the models are ultimately only a medium for these negotiations and are not intended to represent a unique and absolute truth.

The concepts are represented by circles with a title. In the analogy of the garden, they correspond to the soils in which the plants grow. Like actors, they can combine and group together to express a hierarchical dimension or as a Venn diagram set (see section 4.3.1) to signify logical relations.

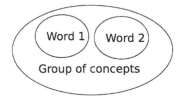

Figure 4.17. *Modeling concepts*

4.3.4. *Relations*

Relations represent the relationships of the physical and conceptual dimensions instantiated by an actor within a given space and time. They are in the form of simple lines which represent a finite state or in the form of arrows to represent a process. These lines represent the roots of the plants. The relations are qualified by a source, a destination and a predicate; they can be considered as RDF triplets (see section 5.1.3.4).

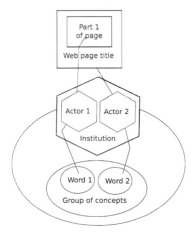

Figure 4.18. *Modeling relations*

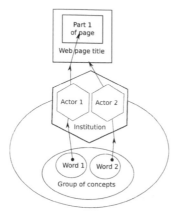

Figure 4.19. *Modeling processes*

It is through relations that we can represent the power of an informational existence to act within an ecosystem of knowledge. This power is obviously shifting and will depend on the spatio-temporal context. Nevertheless, modeling allows us to show its potentialities and to provide analysts with support for their line of questioning and the formalization of their hypotheses. Moreover, this modeling is very useful for calculating the complexity of this "power to act".

4.3.5. *Calculating the complexity of an ecosystem*

From these modeling principles, it is possible to calculate the complexity of a knowledge ecosystem according to generic rules that apply regardless of the knowledge domain concerned. In this way, the comparison of domains in terms of ecosystem complexity and the complexity of views on the ecosystem under analysis becomes possible.

4.3.5.1. *Existential complexity*

According to a principle of fractality, complex informational existences consist of simpler informational existences, but nonetheless built on the same model. The complexity of an informational existence is calculated from the sum of the physical dimension, the actor, the concept and the relations. We note that this complexity increases in relation to the subparts composing the dimensions, that which essentially describes the detail of a dimension. Therefore, to the simple addition of parts, we must add a coefficient of fractality which increases the complexity by multiplying the number of subparts by their level of detail.

For example, if we model a library as a single physical dimension, this existence has a complexity of 1, i.e.: 1 physical dimension * 1 fractal \ level = 1. If we add into the modeling the number of books it contains, we model an additional level of detail and the fractal coefficient changes to 2. The complexity of this new model is calculated by adding the initial complexity 1 and the number of books multiplied by the fractal coefficient: 2. If the library has 100 books, the complexity will be $1 + (100 \times 2) = 201$. The same procedure applies if you add to the model the number of pages in each book, the number of words per page, and the number of characters per word, etc. This example takes into account only the physical dimensions of the ecosystem. It is, of course, necessary to also take into account the calculation for the dimensions of the actors, the concepts and the relations. The latter constitute a special case since there is only one level for the relations, and because these form networks in which one node is not included in another. The computation for the complexity is done on the basis of the number of distinct elements in the 15 possible permutations of the four existential dimensions according to three properties of the relation: the source, the destination and the predicate. To this sum of elements, we add the total sum of ratios for each permutation in order to compute a complexity which, increasing with the number of permutations, decreases with the number of repetitions for the same element in a permutation (for a detailed example of calculation refer to [SZO 17a]).

4.3.5.2. *Complexity of viewpoints*

Parallel to the existential complexity of the knowledge ecosystem, we can calculate the complexity of the analyst's viewpoint of this ecosystem. Indeed, the analysis of a knowledge ecosystem can never be exhaustive, as it is infinitely descriptible in each dimension that composes it. The analyst will have to make choices and as a consequence only take into account part of the ecosystem. If we take the example of the library again, the analyst's point of view does not necessarily take into account all the books, perhaps only one book, or even one sentence in one of the books or even a word. From this, the complexity of his point of view can be calculated and compared with other points of view on the same ecosystem. The complexity index of the viewpoint is calculated by comparing the complexity of the viewpoint with the complexity of the ecosystem. An ideal viewpoint that takes into account the totality of an ecosystem would therefore have an index of 1.

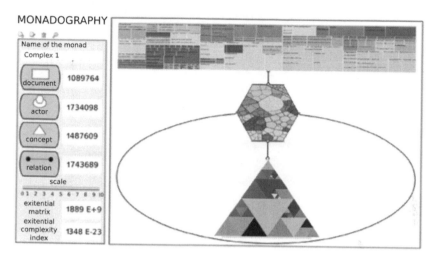

Figure 4.20. *Tools for exploring knowledge ecosystems*

We are working on a prototype platform for exploring knowledge ecosystems that should facilitate modeling and automate the computation of existential complexities and viewpoints. This tool is not yet operational; however, the screenshot (Figure 4.20) gives an idea of the user interface.

5

Web Platform Specifications for Knowledge Ecosystems

This thinking of the knowledge
as movement and emotion
requires in turn a general organology,
wherein sense organs [...] call
for a logical [...] organization.
Bernard Stiegler[1]

One of the central theses of this work
is that knowledge is not an object,
but that it does not apprehend
only through objects
through which it is the interpretation.
Bruno Bachimont[2]

The proliferation of research projects that enter the field of digital humanities goes hand in hand with a proliferation of digital tools, their uses and the availability of data. To organize the chaos of digital traces generated by these practices, the scientific community is working to standardize the formalization of information, notably through the establishment of common languages (TEI, RDF, etc.) and through the creation of accessible and interoperable reference databases (see section 5.1.2.5). In this context, it is

---

1 Translation of quote from http://arsindustrialis.org/desire-and-knowledge-dead-seize-living.
2 Translation of quote from [BAC 07].

fundamental that the work of researchers is able to enrich these databases as simply as possible, without adding additional processing chains that can lead to errors and worse, misuse of the researcher's interpretation. Based on the numerous experiments carried out in this field [JUA 10, LAT 12, GAL 14, TER 15, SZO 15], we propose developing a platform based on long-term references (DBpedia, BnF data, ISNI, symogih, etc.) to provide researchers with the means to graphically model their interpretations. Once modeled, these interpretations are able to enrich the reference databases and provide a calculable material for algorithm classification, sorting and the automatic generation of documents that can notably be used as digital educational resources.

Beyond the simple use of tools or the definition of "good practice", the Web platform for collective intelligence and the methodology that we want to develop have the ambition of integrating the dimensions of teaching into the research processes and the production of educational resources. The aim is to organize the participation of researchers, teachers, students and industrialists in order to create a virtuous cycle for the production of digital educational resources, while respecting the socio-technical ecosystem that makes up the sector of E-education. It is possible to take advantage of the plasticity of digital technology, in partnership with industry, to reinvest in the documents and produce them as multilingual, intercultural educational resources, and thus shed new light on E-educational practices by experimenting with innovative learning methods.

For several years, we have been developing a Web platform called the "Knowledge Garden" or "KG" (*Le jardin des connaissances* or *JDC*), which is dedicated to the management of knowledge ecosystems. This chapter introduces the technical principles for a generic resource management model, the details of implementation choices, and the technical specifications of this platform[3] for data sources, server applications and client applications.

---

3 Link to the GitHub project which manages the developments and use returns: https://github.com/samszo/jardindesconnaissances

5.1. The generic management of resources

We present here the functional justifications and technical specifications for managing the resources that nourish the ecosystem. We propose a model that we conceive as generic, that is, capable of adapting to all knowledge ecosystems, even if we thought it more specific to digital humanities and E-education. In relation to a pharmacological use, the generic term refers here to the idea of a molecular structure passed in the public domain and usable without having to pay rights. We use the generic term in this perspective, and also with the idea that the model we propose allows us to instantiate multiple generations all built following the same "DNA" and which can develop its own characteristics.

The resources available for a knowledge ecosystem are as multiple as they are varied. We will first address the issue of resources which offer non-digital knowledge potential and how the ecosystem can manage them. Second, we will discuss digital resources through a presentation of the different types available on the Web. Finally, we will analyze how to organize ecosystem resources and how this organization leads us to design hybrid databases involving different technologies and data sources.

5.1.1. *Non-digital resources*

Even if today most knowledge is digitized or scannable, there are still fields of knowledge that cannot be translated into 0's and 1's. We support the idea that for the here and now, knowledge is the experimentation of relations between an individual in all of its complexity and a context taken in all of its complexity. If the experience of a text, an image, a video or a sound loses only a minority of its complexity when it passes through a digitized object, other experiences lose the majority of their complexity and thereby lose from the experience its power by stimulating less of the user's power for discernment. In this chapter, we will detail the categories of experiences that are not digitizable, such as taste, "craft" and living things, and then we will present the methods to make this knowledge accessible.

5.1.1.1. *The taste of things*

Whether it is the smell of a rose or the taste of an oyster, it is difficult to digitize this knowledge which, we all know, is not limited to the description of it. The complexity of the relations that an individual has with his own interiority and the context of his existence make it difficult to digitize the taste that focuses in an instant on an "existential precipitate" in the sense understood by chemists, that is, the generation of a substance when pooled from several elements. This type of knowledge therefore passes, in the words of Jean-Jacques Boutaud, by a "sensible grip", that is, by the experimentation in the here and now of a connection between material and emotional elements which depend on factors that are impossible to reproduce as they are linked to both physical and psychological microvariations and societal macrophenomena. The moment of the taste experience therefore passes through a non-numerical "dynamogeny" because:

> "The moment is to be conceived, in its figurative dimension, as a form and even more a process of formation. It is part of an ecology of action in which body language and verbal language are mimed, interacting with the resources available to the actor, in the time and space in which the activity takes place."[4] [BOU 15, p. 29]

5.1.1.2. *Craft as an intuition of experience*

What differentiates a young apprentice from an accomplished craftsman? Simply the practice time that, achieved by the artisan, has allowed him to develop an intuition of experience in order to anticipate problems or solve them more quickly. This is called "craft", a form of "common sense" that guides the activity at each stage of its completion. This knowledge acquired over time is not only logical, but far more intuitive; it allows the craftsman to "feel" what to do without even being able to explain why. It is difficult to digitize this non-formalized knowledge, especially since it would be necessary to record all feedback loops that give the craftsman the means to build his "craft" through a continuum of errors and successes. Should we not take these into account in the design of a knowledge gardening platform? Of course not.

---

4 Translation of French quote.

Two complementary approaches are needed to manage "business" knowledge. The first is to record the stages of this knowledge by offering the user a "mirror" of his activities. By representing the repetitions of the tasks he performs, we can observe the practices for which an actor builds experience, and those which he does not. This history has two main utilities: first, it gives the actor the means for reflexivity on their activity(s), after which they enter in the recommendation algorithm settings which can thus advise on which tasks to concentrate upon in order to balance the experience; the second approach is to identify the actors with the most important experience within a given field of activity so as to put them in connection with the actors who do not have any and who wish to develop these activities.

5.1.1.3. Address the conditions of knowledge

Since the knowledge we just mentioned is not digitizable, how can the platform manage it?

One of the ways is to simply create a directory of activities that allows us to experiment with this knowledge. Another way is to connect the person who wants to know with the person who knows and is able to transmit this knowledge. In the end, the experimenters must be given the means to express the knowledge they have experienced. This last point is fundamental since it conditions the genericity of the ecosystem. Indeed, the expression of feedback nourishes the ecosystem both at the level of the repertoire of activities, and also at the level of the network of experts. All these returns serve both the users, as a reflective mirror of their own practices, and more generally the ecosystem which in turn becomes more complex with each addition of experience, thereby enriching the potentiality of knowledge for each. In order for these feedback loops to turn into a virtuous rather than a vicious circle, the expression of feedback must be confronted with two imperatives:

– the first is to make this expression interoperable and calculable with the entire ecosystem by setting up formal rules for information management (see section 3.2.9);

– the second is not to lock the user in logico-formal expressions but always leave him the possibility of a fluctuation as a result of their own expression. Concretely, rather than expressing a Boolean "Yes"/"No" value in the form of a check box, give priority to a qualitative expression in the form of a cursor that allows us to position them between two poles.

We have just seen how knowledge cannot be digitized because the challenge of reproducing the complex conditions of experimentation is impossible either in the moment (taste) or in the history of its constitution (craft). The generic solution that we advocate can be summed up as follows: the experimentation of knowledge is possible from the moment we create the constraints of expressing this knowledge, even if minimal, such as defining the duration of experimentation.

5.1.2. *Digital resources*

Today, digital resources are the most readily available material with which to feed and grow knowledge ecosystems. In this section, we present some of these resources by showing how they involve varying accessibility policies and levels of complexity.

5.1.2.1. *The document server*

The first and most common sources of digital data are the digital documents that can be found on every computer network. These documents are in multiple formats and dedicated to a wide variety of uses.

First and foremost are the documents we have on our personal or professional machines. These documents, which we put in directory trees, helter-skelter on the desktop or more often than not somewhere we cannot quite remember, constitute our digital memory, the one in which we are primarily responsible since we are at the origin of their creation, and more generally their life cycle. Even if at present, these documents are tending more and more to move from our machines to online storage, in the "clouds" of big servers, the organization of these documents is the first aspect of our knowledge ecosystem. Studies conducted as part of a master 2 training in hypermedia technology [BOU 16] have shown that even in this environment where we are yet to become fully accustomed to the use of computers, few users set up filing strategies to organize their source computer. Their trust in search engines that "know" to find the right file leads them to practice the bare minimum in terms of storage organization, for example, only placing documents on the desktop.

This disempowerment of the user in relation to the organization of these documents is symptomatic of the transfer of power between the user and the algorithm. It is no longer the user who discerns what is specific to the document that becomes generic, the algorithm takes over. This is especially true of today, where the storage of these documents is also left to the responsibility of a mechanistic third party.

5.1.2.2. *RSS feeds*

RSS feeds[5] are one of the better-known and most widely used sources for collecting digital data. Based on XML, RSS is a specification that defines news channels that can be subscribed to so as to inform a person of the latest news being posted on a website. This is often used with a feed aggregator that displays the contents of the feed and provides tools for setting and editing. Notably, RSS feeds can also be exploited with algorithms.

5.1.2.3. *API and Web service*

As described in section 1.3, APIs are one of the keys to ecosystem modeling through their management function of the IT relationships between different ecosystems. The term API, or Application Program Interfaces, defines communication interfaces with and for applications. Less open than LOD (see section 5.1.2.5), APIs are accessible after authentication and sometimes require payment. Among the best known and most used are Google Maps, Twitter, etc. Up until the 2010s, we talked about "MASHUP" to define websites that used APIs, but today the use of this technology is so widespread that the term has slowly disappeared, as proven by the website www.programmableweb.com, which now concentrates its census activity almost exclusively on APIs.

---

5 Link to RSS specifications: http://www.rssboard.org/rss-specification

Perhaps the most iconic example of an API and services platform is Google, which provides Web developers with an API ecosystem via a dedicated platform that covers all information management needs:

– manage access to all Google APIs;

– consult with the documentation;

– learn through tutorials;

– monetize the use of APIs;

– host Web applications;

– sell solutions;

– analyze the dissemination of this information.

The goal of Google, like other companies providing API ecosystems, is obviously to attract the attention of users to increase the economic benefits generated by these information flows [CIT 14]. By offering these services for free and providing all the information needed for their use, a point on which Google is particularly exemplary, these companies capture the power to act as developers, who themselves will capture the attention of users. In the end, these companies multiply the growth of their ecosystem by promoting the emergence of new applications in their own environment.

The difficulty of this type of application is that they are dependent on the ecosystem of these societies that can evolve or even disappear, and thus render completely obsolete an application that will disappear from existence because it is no longer adapted to its environment. Here again, the analogy of the ecosystem is particularly relevant for thinking about this type of problem as it relates to the life cycle of a service.

In the Knowledge Garden, we have developed our own APIs to manage the flow of information between our application servers and clients as simply as possible. These APIs are open for consultation except those that modify the information stored within our databases, and for which authentication is requested. We also use external APIs to deport features or to retrieve information from users of other ecosystems, for example:

Name	Uses	URL
Alchemy	Keyword extractor	http://www.alchemyapi.com
Aylien	Keyword extractor	https://api.aylien.com/api/v1/
CEPT	Keyword extractor	https://cept.3scale.net/docs
Diigo	Web resource annotation	https://secure.diigo.com
Enseignement Sup	Open Data Engine for Higher Education and French research	https://data.enseignementsup-recherche.gouv.fr/api/records/1.0/search
Flickr	Social network photo sharing	
Google Books	Book platform	
Google Calendar	Calendar management	
Google Contacts	Contact management	
Google Data	Data platform	
Google Drive	Document platform	
Google Knowledge Graph	Open database	
Google mail	Mailbox	
Google URL	URL shortener	https://developers.google.com/url-shortener/v1/getting_started
Hal	Scientifc article repository	https://hal-univ-paris8.archives-ouvertes.fr/stat/ajaxdata
Istex	Research data	https://api.istex.fr
Open Calais	Keyword extractor	http://www.opencalais.com/documentation/opencalais-documentation
ParlTrack	Management of the democratic processes of the European Parliament	
P2Net	Patent management	http://patent2netv2.vlab4u.info/
Rmngp	Semantic data of national museums	https://docs.art.rmngp.fr/
ScoopIt	Collaborative management of interest lists	http://www.scoop.it/dev/api/1/intro
Textalytics	Keyword extractor	https://textalytics.com/core/topics-info#doc
Yahoo Content Analysis	Keyword extractor	http://developer.yahoo.com/search/content/V2/contentAnalysis.html
Zemanta	Keyword extractor	http://developer.zemanta.com/
Zotero	Bibliography management	https://api.zotero.org

Table 5.1. *List of APIs external to the Knowledge Garden*

5.1.2.4. *Web scraping*

An important source for constituting digital data comes from the automatic extraction of the structured content present in web pages. Today, almost all HTML pages visible on the Web are built from algorithms that search databases for content so as to format them according to a predefined visualization model. Web scraping uses the visualization model to categorize and extract data. For example, Figure 5.1 shows the structure of a web page dedicated to monitoring science, which we used to categorize content and extract data necessary to analyze the locations of information and communication science worldwide [HAC 14]. The collected corpus consists of data extracted automatically from the website dedicated to monitoring the technology of French embassies. In order to extract the data, we have listed the bulletins in chronological order so as to record nearly 70,000 web pages.

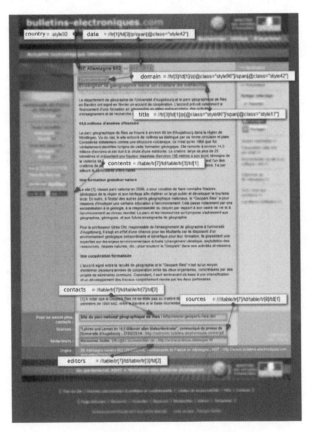

Figure 5.1. *Categorizing a page for a scraping algorithm*

As this list shows, we have developed several extraction models:

Name	Uses	URL
ADIT	Science Monitoring Bulletins	http://www.adit.fr/
Amazon	Bibliographic information	http://www.amazon.com
Cairn	Scientific articles	https://www.cairn.info/
CNRTL[6]	*Centre national de ressources textuelles et lexicales*	http://www.cnrtl.fr/
Decitre	Bibliographic information	http://www.decitre.fr
IISI[7]	International Statistical Institute	http://isi.cbs.nl/glossary/
Bup8	Paris 8 BU Stream	http://catalogue.bu.univ-paris8.fr/cgi-bin/koha/opac-main.pl

Table 5.2. *List of scraping models*

The main difficulties with data sources of this type are: first, the specificity of the extraction structures that need to adapt to each data source, and second, the non-sustainability of the extraction structures that are dependent on a change in the design of the data sources. One way around these two problems is to save the web pages in a database in which the original data source and the data specifically categorized for retrieval will both be stored.

5.1.2.5. *Linked Open Data*

As a result of W3C initiatives and Tim Berners-Lee's open data sharing perspectives, one of the most important data sources of today are the databases linked to each other by common references. Linked data sets, known as Linked Open Data (LOD), represent millions of pieces of information that grow exponentially each day. At the heart of LOD is a particular formalism, the Resource Description Framework or RDF (see section 5.1.3.4). This format is used to define ontologies and allows for the very precise description of knowledge networks. To query this data, two protocols predominate: OAI and SPARQL.

---

6 French National Center for Textual and Lexical Resources
7 *Institut international de statistique*

5.1.2.6. *OAI*

Open Archives Initiative (OAI) is historically the first open data provisioning protocol[8]. The OAI protocol has specifications that provide data stores and ways to harvest them, through six basic actions[9], in order to obtain:

– a specific record: GetRecord;

– the description of a data store: Identify;

– the identifier list for each record: ListIdentifiers;

– the list of metadata formats: ListMetadataFormats;

– a registration list: ListRecords;

– the list of store structures: ListSets.

We note that this protocol does not provide actions for saving, updating or deleting data. Data providers are therefore solely responsible for the quality and durability of the data, positioning themselves as guarantors of "immortal" references. In this sense, OAI stores, even if they use a vocabulary derived from agriculture (metadata harvesting), are closed ecosystems that limit interactions with other ecosystems.

5.1.2.7. *SPARQL access point*

Today, open data makes it possible for SPARQL access points[10] to interact with their data. Far more complex than OAI, SPARQL access points provide a very advanced query language for querying linked data stored in an RDF triplestore. For example, it is possible with a SPARQL query to query the BNF[11] data to retrieve all the documents where Victor Hugo is the author of the text, and, if applicable, the attached works[12]:

---

8 For a detailed chronology of initiatives for the opening of the data, see http://oad. simmons.edu/oadwiki/Timeline

9 For the detailed specifications of the protocol, see http://www.openarchives.org/OAI/

10 For an assesment of the available access points, see http://sparqles.ai.wu.ac.at/

11 For detailed examples: http://data.bnf.fr/docs/doc_requetes_data.pdf

12 The result of this query is consultable here: https://goo.gl/qKBrM8

```
  SELECT DISTINCT ?doc ?oeuvre ?titre WHERE
{?doc marcrel:aut
<http://data.bnf.fr/ark:/12148/cb11907966z#
foaf:Person>. Optional {?oeuvre
rdarelationships:expressionOfWork ?doc ; rdfs:label ?titre.}}
```

Box 5.1. *SPARQL query on the BnF data*

We note that even if the SPARQL protocol allows for the addition and updating of data, the majority of access points do not allow this kind of request. Once again, it can be understood that the institutions guaranteeing data do not allow anyone to create, modify or delete their references. However, this can cause problems, for example, when researchers discover errors or gaps in the data they are consulting. Indeed, it is often very long, if not impossible to modify such data. In order to overcome this problem to allow experts to modify reference data, it is possible to set up databases that will collect the annotations of contributors in an open and interoperable format, such as those proposed by the open annotation workgroup[13].

In order to power our Knowledge Garden platform, we have implemented several SPARQL entry points in order to collect reference data. Here is the list:

Name	Uses	URL
DataBNF	Bibliographic data	http://data.bnf.fr/sparql/
DBpedia	Encyclopedia	http://fr.dbpedia.org/sparql
UNESCO	Thesaurus education	http://skos.um.es/sparql/index.php

Table 5.3. *List of SPARQL entry points*

5.1.2.8. *Authentication server*

Of the information sources that organize information ecosystems, authentication servers are very important as they are the gateways that filter entry into the ecosystem and define the rights being granted to the user when they return. Today, rather than taking responsibility for setting up its own user management system, many sites now use third parties to authenticate

13 http://www.openannotation.org/

individuals and manage their rights. Whether through GAFAM, institutions such as universities[14] or free platforms like OpenId[15], it is possible to use these authentication platforms to validate an individual's identity and rights.

If the interest for an actor wishing to make a Web application available is obvious in terms of development cost and especially in terms of connection to important community networks, this results in an implicit acceptance of the rules of confidentiality, management of the platform authentication and therefore participation in a particular ecosystem. This is one of the main challenges of GAFAM, which offers these authentication services in order to grow their own ecosystem, by letting the millions of developers who use these services to invent new features and thereby capture, at the lowest cost, the attention of Internet users.

5.1.2.9. *Content Management System*

In just a few years, Content Management Systems (CMS) have become indispensable tools for Web developing by enabling multimedia content to be put online without having to know a single line of computer code. These tools are often used as a basis for a digital Web device because they offer the usual information management features (see section 5.3.3). There are now several thousand different CMS, the best known being WordPress[16], Drupal[17], Joomla[18] or SPIP[19] widely used in French public administrations. These tools differ in the technologies they use and the functionality they offer[20], but the basic principle of their operation remains very similar. It consists of connecting three layers of information: a database, a "back office" and a "front office". The database is specific to each CMS both in terms of the technologies used and its structure, and it is invisible to users except for developers who want to extend the functionality of the CMS. The "back office" provides editing tools for identified users so that, according to the rights they have, they are able to organize, create, update or delete the content being stored in the database. The "front office" is the layer of information that makes the content visible to all Internet users, most often

---

14 For an example of a CAS authentication system see: https://www.apereo.org/projects/cas
15 http://goo.gl/kI2aa
16 https://wordpress.org/
17 https://www.drupal.com/
18 https://www.joomla.com/
19 http://www.spip.net/
20 Main CMS with analysis grid, http://www.cmsmatrix.org/matrix

through a "theme" (see section 5.2.4.1.1) that the CMS administrator has chosen among those that are available to them, free or for a fee.

5.1.3. *Management of digital resources*

Overall, the management of digital resources begins with the modeling of an information structure that defines how data will be constructed, with what characteristics and at what levels of accuracy. The resources will then be described according to this model so as to make data manipulable by algorithms and/or humans. The compatibility between data modeling and the purpose of their manipulation is the crucial point of the management of digital resources and requires a double expertise, both in terms of the understanding of the aims and the data modeling needed for this.

Digital data can be manipulated by programs that can be modeled and manipulated using four basic actions: Create, Read, Update and Delete (or CRUD). There are different technologies and languages to perform these actions. We will not enter into an expert debate into which is the better technology, since the solutions are multiple and the potential applications are infinite. Nonetheless, it is important to remember that these technologies fall into three main categories [FER 14]:

– query language: SQL, SPARQL and Natural Language Interfaces (NLIs);

– navigation structure: file system and hypertext;

– interactive view: e.g. facets and OLAP.

To evaluate these technologies, the questions that designers must ask themselves are as follows [FER 14]:

– expressiveness: to which type of question can one answer?

– confidence: how much confidence can be attributed to the answers?

– accessibility: how easy is it for the user to understand the questions, answers and data control interfaces?

– support: are users guided in the expression of their needs?

– specificity: does the support correspond to current data?

– scalability: how much data can be managed?

5.1.3.1. *Key – value*

NoSQL technologies have emerged with the proliferation of data centers for which paradigms other than those of relational databases (see section 5.1.3.6) are necessary, in particular to meet the performance needs of big data. At the same time, Web applications and the increasingly intensive use of web services and JavaScript have helped to compete with relational databases. There are now many NoSQL DBMS[21], for which we will provide detail only on the most basic principles.

The simplest principle of NoSQL data management is the creation of a one-dimensional array that associates a key and a value. We find the organization in a table where each column designates a key and each line a value for this key. This information storage format is very efficient for writing and reading data, but it is very resource-intensive when it is necessary to update or delete a particular value. On the contrary, the simplicity of this principle makes it easy to create data files with only one character to separate the columns. The best known of these characters is the comma "," which gave the generic name for this type of file: CSV (Comma-Separated Values), for example:

---

surname, name, birthday, work 1,work 2, work 3
Zappa, Franck, 21/12/1940, Freak Out, Uncle Meat, Yellow Shark
Gillian, Terry, 22/11/1940, The Baron of Münchhausen, Brazil, Zero Theorem
Giraud, Jean, 08/05/1938, Blueberry, L'Incal, Le Monde d'Edena

---

Box 5.2. *CSV sample data*

As we can see, the principle of structuring data is very simple, but it is problematic when you want to add information. The example in Box 5.2 allows you to organize three works for each author, where if you want to put a fourth, you will need to add a new column "work 4", but if you want to describe more precisely a work by adding, for example, its date of creation, you will have to add as many columns as there are works, which is not very economical in terms of storing information, especially given that it will be very difficult to develop an algorithm that anticipates this type of update.

---

21 http://nosql-database.org/

5.1.3.2. *XML*

XML is another NoSQL data organization tool that operates according to three basic concepts: hierarchy, node and attribute. XML is a language for structuring data with tags by defining parent and child node hierarchies from a first root node. Each node will be characterized by attributes operating according to the key value principle, for example:

```
<root>
    <artist surname="Zappa" name="Franck" birthday="21/12/1940" >
        <works>
            <work>Freak Out</work>
            <work>Uncle Meat</work>
            <work>Yellow Shark</work>
        <works>
    </artist>
    <artist surname="Gillian" name="Terry" birthday="22/11/1940" >
        <works>
            <work>Brazil</work>
            <work>The Baron of Münchhausen </work>
            <work>Zero Theorem</work>
        <works>
    </artist>
    <artist surname="Giraud" name="Jean" birthday="08/05/1938" >
        <works>
            <work>Blueberry</work>
            <work>Incal</work>
            <work>The World of Edena</work>
        <works>
    </artist>
</root>
```

Box 5.3. *Examples of XML data*

The simplicity of this notation format and the possibility of editing schemas to verify the syntax ensures it is a great success, specifically to specify derived languages dedicated to particular uses, e.g. the SVG for vector drawing, OWL for the definition of ontology, OAI for open archives and TEI for encoding digital documents[22]. One of the problems of this language is its heaviness, because unlike the CSV in which the data are categorized only once for each column, XML repeats the key of each category for each of these values. On the contrary, it is easier to add

22 Here is a non-exhaustive list of XML-based languages: https://en.wikipedia.org/wiki/List_of_XML_

information that can be automatically taken into account by an algorithm. Despite this additional flexibility of XML over CSV, CRUD activities are not as efficient as within relational databases.

5.1.3.3. JSON

Despite some enthusiasm in the 1980s and 1990s, object databases did not meet their expected success, particularly because of the predominance of SQL and its perfect integration into object-oriented languages. On the contrary, over the past 10 years, JSON[23], a computer object notation language, has met with great success. Using a very simple and non-extensible syntax, far less verbose than XML, JSON is increasingly used to exchange data on the Web in combination with JavaScript programming language and AJAX[24] data transport methods. Here, for example, is a list of civilities described in JSON:

```
[
    {surname :"Zappa", name :"Franck", birthday :"21/12/1940"}
    {surname :"Gillian", name :"Terry", birthday :"22/11/1940"}
    {surname :"Giraud", name :"Jean" ; birthday :"08/05/1938"}
]
```

Box 5.4. *Example of JSON data*

If indeed this language is extremely useful for developing dynamic and interactive human–machine interfaces, it is nevertheless difficult to use it in order to make complex queries between objects that relational databases allow for.

5.1.3.4. Ontological triplet

Ontological formalism has become one of the cornerstones of digital resource management and for its definition, storage, indexing, querying and representation [SZO 17a]. The genericity of the ontological process is based on a basic semantic brick, the triplet: subject, predicate and object. This three-dimensional organization of information involves elements that maintain a close entanglement relationship as shown by Douglas Hofstadter in the following representation:

---

23 JavaScript Object notation: https://fr.wikipedia.org/wiki/JavaScript_Object_Notation
24 https://fr.wikipedia.org/wiki/Ajax_(informatique)

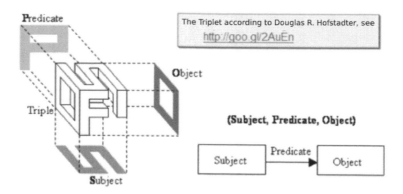

Figure 5.2. *Ontological triplet*

Following the principles of the triplet and based on the Resource Description Framework (RDF), specifications have been developed in order to define languages for ontology modeling. The best known is undoubtedly OWL, whose success has developed alongside the tools dedicated to its use, such as Protégé[25]. However, there are other languages like SKOS (Simple Knowledge Organization System) dedicated to the organization of knowledge or FOAF (Friend of a Friend) dedicated to the description of people and their relationships.

Because it is very simple and very generic, RDF formalism makes it easy to link information coming from different sources and then to design reasoners that are then able to exploit this data autonomously. This is, for example, what we experienced in the OntoStats research project, led under the direction of Jean-Marc Meunier[26]. In this project, we realize an ontology of statistics with which we index educational resources and their uses. These very precise and highly structured categorizations will serve as a basis for Recommender Systems, which will facilitate the learning of statistics.

5.1.3.5. *Relational databases*

Relational Database Managers (RDBs), most often SQL, are the most commonly found today because of the age and robustness of these technologies, and also because there are very effective tools to manage this

25 http://protege.stanford.edu/
26 http://www.ontostats.univ-paris8.fr/

type of database and set up CRUD management using frameworks[27]. Besides the two industrial solutions, Microsoft SQL Server and Oracle, free database managers like MySQL have allowed many developers to create client–server applications. The best known is probably Content Management Systems (CMS). These free DBMS provide simple solutions so as to publish dynamic content on the Web, but not on the Web 2.0.

Relational databases are built from tables that define information structures in the form of columns corresponding to a property. For example, the "*Auteur*" (author) table is structured by the columns: "*Nom*" (surname), "*Prenom*" (first name), "*date_naissance*" (date of birth), etc. One of the fundamental principles of these databases is to make sure that each row within a table can be uniquely identified. Most often, a column is used in which a number is stored and increases with each line addition. This uniqueness of the line is fundamental from a technical point of view, because it allows for the creation of relations between the tables, for example to create a relation between an author and a list of works.

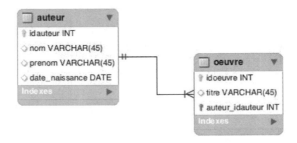

Figure 5.3. *Simple model of an SQL database*

We note, however, that from a conceptual point of view, this technical constraint of the uniqueness of each line is attached to the idea that there is a unique way of describing the data. This influence of data uniqueness is reflected in the very conception of information systems, which often neglects the possibility that two users of the system may have two different descriptions of the same data, without even mentioning the evolution over time of these interpretations. Whatever the conceptual limits imposed by the computer systems for their smooth operation and the problems of cultural interoperability [FAV 16], it is fortunately always possible to adapt them so

27 For example: Zend, Symphony and Laravel.

as to manage the multiplicity of interpretations, by adding to the diagram of the database an intermediate table which allows multiple "n – n" relationships:

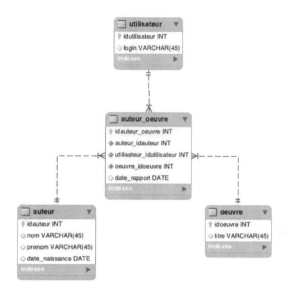

Figure 5.4. *Multi-interpretation SQL model*

The first major interest of relational databases concerns, as we have already said, the robustness of solutions that have been available for a long time and are controlled by many people. The second interest concerns the compartmentalization of knowledge, universal in generic schemes. Indeed, these databases offer a closed universe that can be represented by schemas or scripts, which allows them to be duplicated and multiply the uses. This is, for example, what CMS does (see section 5.1.2.9), where each has their own schema to handle a multitude of data. Having a closed universe allows the expert to develop over time an intuitive knowledge of his database, which is very useful for evaluating the relevance of the results that sometimes send very complex queries.

5.2. Principles for developing a Web ecosystem platform

After this general presentation of the resources, let us detail how to manage them by presenting the development principles that we used to create the Knowledge Garden Web platform. We are inspired by the software architecture of "Models, Views, Controllers" (*Modèles, Vues, Contrôleurs* or MVC) which is today very widely used. This architecture consists of three independent layers that globally correspond to three types of IT activities that are often related to different trades. The "models" layer is supported by Database Administrators (DBAs), the "controllers" layer by "back-end" developers, and the "views" layer by UX (User Experience) and UI (User Interface) specialists. Depending on the size of the project, these three activities will be carried out by one or more people.

In this chapter, we are interested in these three main layers of a Web platform, starting with the "models" and more specifically the databases that are at the heart of the platform. We then discuss the "controllers" layer by presenting the principles used to control the ecosystem at the level of the algorithmic manipulation of flows and their editorial management. Finally, we present the "views" layer by detailing the technologies which we use to develop interfaces that will allow users to garden ecosystems.

5.2.1. *Databases as a model of the ecosystem*

Databases are at the heart of the semantic organization of knowledge ecosystems and their CRUD management (see section 5.1.3). We focused on the dynamic dimension of ecosystems by proposing a model oriented toward the notion of information flow, which leads us to consider the information recorded in the database as being always transient between two states. In the platform that we put forward, in order to define specific ecological niches, we have chosen to multiply the databases to facilitate their implementation, increase performance and make data interoperable, regardless of the ecosystem domain. We have opted for a generic database model that we present in this chapter by emphasizing six essential points of ecosystem data management: hybridization, genericity, geolocation, historization, hierarchization and inclusion of the third party.

5.2.1.1. *Hybrid databases*

We have seen above that in practice there are different ways to manage digital information (see section 5.1.3), and it turns out that these means can be combined in a database that combines SQL and NoSQL to have the advantages of both technologies. The term "mashup" is often used to define this type of application that mixes several technological "ingredients" to obtain a "mashup". We prefer the term "hybrid" which defines the same type of situation, but in the context of organizing that which is living with reference to this ancestral practice of making hybrids between plants or animals in order to obtain the best attributes of each selected organism. In this hybrid organization, the SQL database will be the privileged management space for storing information and executing complex queries, for example, when it comes to grouping data or mass calculations. NoSQL technologies are used to organize information flow exchanges and to manage the complex setting of screens used by users to manipulate data.

Let us take the concrete example of the tool for mapping the influences of which we develop the prototype (see section C.1.1). In this tool, the hybridization of data is characterized by the organization of the following flows:

– a MySQL database (see section 5.2.1.2) for managing users and managing transient data states;

– CSV data from a Google form[28] corresponding to the concepts that users have chosen to define their influence networks;

– JSON data to set the display of data tables in the application;

– RDF data from the BNF[29] SPARQL server to retrieve perennial and interoperable information;

– HTML data from data.bnf, Gallica, Wikipedia, etc. to view the reference information;

– IMAGE data from Gallica to record the details of a digitized archive;

---

28 Link of the form: https://goo.gl/tjjzYn
29 Link of the SPARQL access point: http://data.bnf.fr/sparql/

– JSON data from the Google Knowledge Graph[30] service to retrieve perennial and interoperable information;

– OBJECT data from the Google_Service_Books service to retrieve information about books;

– Cartographic data from Open Street Map[31] for the geolocation of information;

– Open Annotation RDF data to export influence networks in an interoperable format.

According to manipulation needs, the data will be stored, either simply as a document in the form of links, in a binary or textual form, or in a more complex manner as a particular ecosystem modeled on the four dimensions of document, actor, design and relation. For example, the graphical creation of an influence network with the tool will generate both a JSON-type document corresponding to the graphical configuration of the network and a set of data corresponding to the ecosystem model for this network. The graphical data will be used to display the network state and allow its manipulation (see section 4.2), the ecosystem data will be used to relate this model with other models for the ecosystem to calculate, for example, development recommendations [KEM 14].

As we can see, the complexity of hybrid data management illustrates the need to use a more complex organizational paradigm rather than a more complex architecture, in order to privilege the live aspects of this data and their manipulation.

5.2.1.2. *Generic model*

Our main goal in modeling our platform database was to be able to handle all parts or subparts of a knowledge ecosystem. In the same way that the CMS databases (see section 5.1.2.9) organize the content of an infinite number of domains, we want to make our ecosystem management generic. Starting from the theoretical principles (Chapter 3: Fundamental Principles for Modeling an Existence) and the graphical rules that we have defined, we have modeled a generic database whose schema is presented in Figure 5.5.

---

30 https://kgsearch.googleapis.com
31 http://osm.org

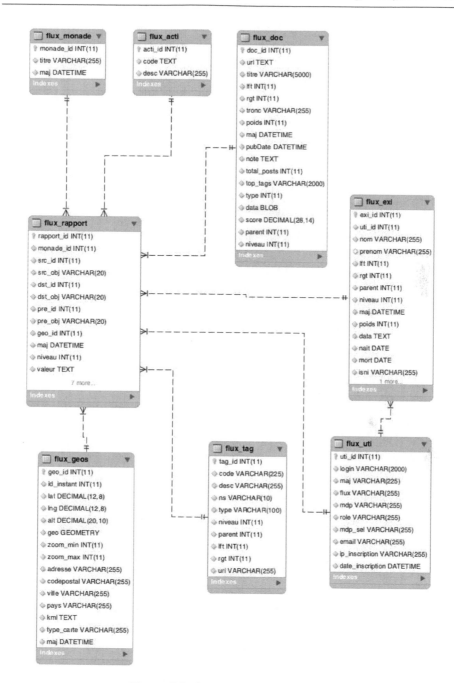

Figure 5.5. *Generic database model*

This database model takes up the principle of the four fundamental objects of graphic modeling (documents, actors, designs and relations) by grouping it in an existential entity that we call a "monad" [LAT 13] and associating with each of these objects a dedicated table:

– "monad" objects are recorded in the "flux_monade" table; they correspond to a particular ecological niche defined by a name and all the relations that constitute it. The monad is considered here as the unique formalization of a particular existence;

– the "documents" objects are managed by the table "doc_flow" in which are stored the information concerning the physical dimensions of the existences as well as the parts that compose them (see section 5.2.1.5). In this table are recorded, for example, the web pages that make up the ecosystem, both in the form of a hypertext link ("URL" field) and in a binary form where possible ("data" field) in order to be able to work on the ecosystem even without connecting to the Web;

– the "actors" objects are registered in the table "flux_exi" and described by basic information: "surname", "first name", date of birth "birth" and date of death "death". We note that a specific field is available to store the ISNI number of the actor so as to facilitate interoperability with Linked Open Data. It should also be noted that a hierarchy of actors can be defined, for example, in the case of an institution, which is considered as a "father" actor and its members as "child" actors (see section 5.2.1.5);

– the "concept" objects are saved in the table "flux_tag" with reference to the practice of indexing contents by a keyword. The tags are stored in the form of a reduced character string ("code" field), a description ("desc" field) and, if necessary, a link to an URI giving more information on this tag. This last field is used to facilitate data modeling, but in full respect of the model, the link to a resource that enriches the description of a concept should rather be stored as a document and then linked to the concept with a relation;

– the "relations" objects are stored in the "flux_rapport" table following a dynamic ternary model that uses the triplet principle (see section 5.1.3.4): source, destination and predicate. To obtain a completely generic model, each dimension of this triplet is defined by an object type ("src_obj", "dst_obj", "pre_obj") and by its identifier ("src_id", "dst_id", "pre_id"); it is therefore possible to create networks of relationships between all objects in the database. We note that this modeling principle makes it possible to model supergraphs in instances where one of the dimensions of the triplet is a ratio ("dst_obj" = ratio), or even to model hypergraphs in instances where one of the dimensions is a graph ("dst_obj" = monad). The difficulty of these models is in understanding the semantic and cognitive implications of these extremely complex graphs.

5.2.1.3. *Geolocalization*

Spatio-temporal characteristics are the fundamental dimensions of an ecosystem of knowledge. In the next chapter, we will deal with the issue of data historization, focusing here on the management of geolocation data.

Geolocation of knowledge ecosystem data is supported in a dedicated "flux_geos" table. This table is used to store different types of geographic information:

– postal address: composed of four fields allowing for the break down of information and thus facilitating treatments according to the different levels of scale (address, postal code, city and country);

– geographic triplet: three fields are available to manage the three primary geographic dimensions: latitude, longitude and altitude;

– cartography: a field is dedicated to the type of map (satellite, physical, road, etc.), two other fields are used to record cartographic data which serve in particular to define complex geographical objects such as zonings, borders, elevations, etc. These two fields are:

- "geo" type geometry[32] to calculate geographic data directly with the database;

- "kml" to store data as XML data with respect to the KML standard[33].

---

32 https://dev.mysql.com/doc/refman/5.7/en/spatial-datatypes.html
33 https://developers.google.com/kml/documentation/

From this table, the platform can handle any type of information for geolocation, but other geographic information can also be stored in the "doc_flow" table, for example, to keep data in the Geo-JSON[34] format.

5.2.1.4. *Historization*

The historization of data refers to three complementary approaches: that of the temporality of the actions performed in the database; that of the historical evolution of the existences composing the ecosystem; and that of the management of historical data.

It seems important to us to be able to manage the temporal evolutions of an ecosystem, in particular to evaluate dynamics or the contrary, stagnations, and also to calculate the performances of the system in order to know, for example, the time taken for the execution of an algorithm. The database model that we propose manages the historicity of the actions carried out in the ecosystem by means of a "maj" field present in all the tables. Its value is updated automatically after each action on the database. This field allows us, for example, to know from which date a data has not been modified, or to know the most recent data. At the same time, an "acti_flow" table makes it possible to manage the actions that are carried out in the ecosystem and to relate these actions with the other objects of the ecosystem: actor, document, design and relation.

As an example, we have implemented the automatic import of the monitoring that we do with the Diigo[35] tool. The data we retrieve via the API is stored in the database using a simple algorithm that records the documents, the tags and the annotations linked to it[36]. From the data stored in the database, it becomes possible to make queries, for example, to know the import performance numbers for documents and tags over the month of January 2017:

---

34 http://geojson.org/
35 https://www.diigo.com/user/luckysemiosis
36 For more details, see the PHP algorithm here: https://github.com/samszo/jardindesco nnaissances/blob/master/library/Flux/Diigo

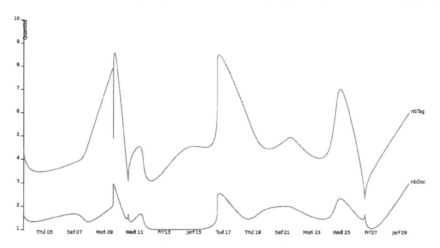

Figure 5.6. *Performance for importing Diigo feeds*

In parallel with this historization of the events for the ecosystem, the database makes it possible to follow the historical evolution of the existences composing the ecosystem. What is at stake is no longer the historization of events in the ecosystem, as we explained in the previous section, but the historical dynamics of existences. From the same ecological niche shown in Figure 5.6, namely the web documents we tagged with Diigo, we created the graph shown in Figure 5.7, which shows the evolution in recent years of our use of the tag "ecosystemeinfo" by quantifying the number of documents we have categorized in relation to information ecosystems.

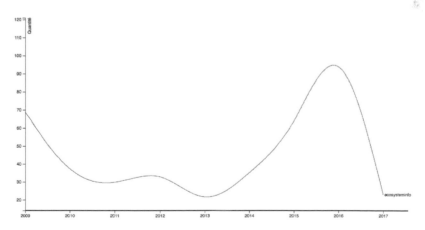

Figure 5.7. *Historical evolution of the "ecosysteminfo" tag*

The flexibility of the model makes it possible to store any type of temporal information by creating a relationship between a key word and another object of the model. For example, to manage the life cycles of a document, it is possible to create the keywords corresponding to each step of the cycle and to store in the "value" field of the "flux_rapport" table, the corresponding date and time at this stage. For example, in the body of documents we categorized with Diigo, we defined life cycles that correspond to the status returned in the HTTP header when querying the document's URL[37]. The retention of these statuses in the database allows us, for example, to know the historical evolution for each document status:

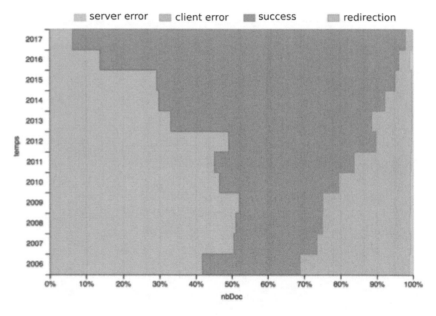

Figure 5.8. *Historical evolution of the HTTP status*

Concerning knowledge ecosystems in the field of historical research, what matters is not only the life cycle of the document, but also the historical period that the document deals with. In addition to managing the publication dates, the historical periods which the document describes are an integral

37 For a list of HTTP statuses, see: https://en.wikipedia.org/wiki/List_of_HTTP_codes

part of the historization. While the computer management of dates is not a problem, as these are now synchronized globally since the adoption of Coordinated Universal Time (UTC[38]), it is not the same for the historical periods that in order to be interoperable should refer to common timelines like the one proposed by the Kronobase[39] site or domain ontologies like those proposed by the Simogih[40] project. From these references, it is possible to enrich the ecosystem of interoperable historical data through a dendrochronological interface that creates the relationship between a document and a historical period.

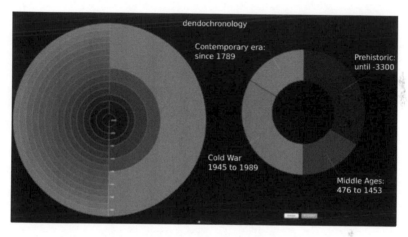

Figure 5.9. *Interface for selecting historical periods*

5.2.1.5. *Prioritization*

The four basic dimensions of modeling that we have described above (documents, actors, designs and relations) are all hierarchical, that is, they can be decomposed into smaller elements or aggregated into an element that encompasses them all.

If XML or JSON are well adapted to hierarchical modeling, it is not the same for relational databases for which specific strategies must be

---

38 https://fr.wikipedia.org/wiki/Temps_universel_coordonn%C3%A9
39 http://www.kronobase.org/
40 http://symogih.org/

implemented. The common way to manage a hierarchy in a relational database is to store the identifier of the "parent" element in the object which you want to prioritize. This is what we did by adding a "parent" field for each of the tables concerned. However, this type of simple strategy poses a real problem when it is necessary to recover the complete hierarchical tree. In fact, in order to retrieve the offspring of an element with an SQL query, it is necessary to make links for each "child" generation. The examples of SQL queries below shows how the query will become more complex as we want to display new offspring. We will take as example the administrative organization for teaching in a university:

```
SELECT p.nom AS Université
    , p1.nom AS TRU
FROM flux_exi AS p
LEFT JOIN flux_exi AS p1 ON p1.parent = p.exi_id
WHERE p.nom = 'Paris8';
```

Box 5.5. *SQL to display the Teaching and Research Unit (TRU) of a university*

University	TRU
Paris 8	MITSIC
Paris 8	Law
Paris 8	Psychology
...	...

Table 5.4. *The TRU of a university*

```
SELECT p.nom AS Université
    , p1.nom AS TRU
    , p2.nom AS Département
FROM flux_exi AS p
LEFT JOIN flux_exi AS p1 ON p1.parent = p.exi_id
LEFT JOIN flux_exi AS p2 ON p2.parent = p1.exi_id
WHERE p.nom = 'Paris8';
```

Box 5.6. *SQL to display the TRU departments of a university*

University	TRU	Department
Paris 8	MITSIC	Computing
Paris 8	MITSIC	Mathematics
Paris 8	MITSIC	Digital Humanities
...	...	...

Table 5.5. *The TRU departments of a university*

```
SELECT p.nom AS Université
    , p1.nom AS TRU
    , p2.nom AS Département
    , p3.nom AS Formations
FROM flux_exi AS p
LEFT JOIN flux_exi AS p1 ON p1.parent = p.exi_id
LEFT JOIN flux_exi AS p2 ON p2.parent = p1.exi_id
LEFT JOIN flux_exi AS p3 ON p3.parent = p2.exi_id
WHERE p.nom = 'Paris8';
```

Box 5.7. *SQL to display the TRU departmental courses of a university*

University	TRU	TRU	Departments
Paris 8	MITSIC	Digital Humanities	THYP
Paris 8	MITSIC	Digital Humanities	NET
Paris 8	MITSIC	Digital Humanities	CEN
...	...	...	...

Table 5.6. *The TRU department courses of a university*

In addition to the problem of the query's complexity, this prioritization strategy poses another problem, that of genericity. Indeed, the request is dependent on the number of hierarchical levels which we want to display. We will not be able to add new hierarchical levels except through changing this request and thus deploying a new version of the application which uses it.

In order to avoid these two problems related to the hierarchization through a "parent" field, one solution is to implement a recursive algorithm to dynamically retrieve the entire hierarchy by searching for "children" at each hierarchical level. However, this solution poses a problem when we wish to make calculations on the hierarchy directly in the database or when we wish to create links between several branches of the hierarchy.

In order to meet all of our hierarchical modeling and computing needs on these hierarchies, we have adopted a strategy that uses a hierarchical nesting model as a complement to the traditional "parent" field prioritization strategy[41]. The principle of this method is to create nested containers whose boundaries are defined from left to right by digital sequences. These sequences are calculated by an algorithm and stored in the database for each element of the hierarchy in a "lft" field for the number on the left and in a "rgt" field for the number on the right. To facilitate processing, we added a "level" field that stores the depth of the element in the hierarchy. Here, for example, is a representation of the university administrative hierarchy following this model:

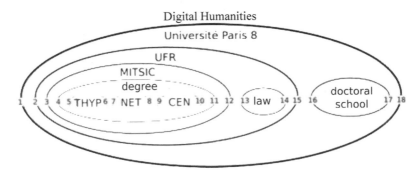

Figure 5.10. *Nested bubble hierarchy*

---

41 For a detailed explanation of this method, see: http://mikehillyer.com/articles/managing-hierarchical-data-in-mysql

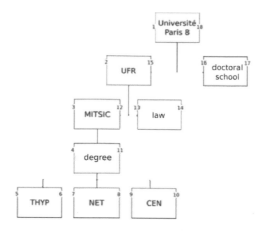

Figure 5.11. *Nested tree hierarchy*

With this model, it becomes easier to explore the hierarchy, for example, to display:

– the complete list of a hierarchy:

```
SELECT e.nom, e.niveau
FROM flux_exi AS e
LEFT JOIN flux_exi AS p
  ON e.lft BETWEEN p.lft AND p.rgt
WHERE p.nom = 'Paris8'
ORDER BY e.lft;
```

Box 5.8. *SQL of a nested hierarchy*

Name	Level
Paris 8	1
TRU	2
MITSIC	3
Formations (Training)	4
THYP	5
NET	5
CEN	5
Droit (Law)	3
Ecole doctorale (Doctoral School)	2

Table 5.7. *List of administrative levels of a French university*

– the full path of an element of the hierarchy:

```
SELECT p.nom, p.niveau
FROM flux_exi AS e
LEFT JOIN flux_exi AS p
  ON e.lft BETWEEN p.lft AND p.rgt
WHERE e.nom = 'THYP'
ORDER BY p.lft;
```

Box 5.9. *SQL for the full path of an element of the hierarchy*

Name	Level
Paris 8	1
TRU	2
MITSIC	3
Trainings	4
THYP	5

Table 5.8. *Path to an element of the hierarchy*

Although this strategy makes it easier to display hierarchies, it is a little more complex when you add, update or delete an element of the hierarchy. Indeed, after each action on the database, it is necessary to update the "lft" and "rgt" fields for each element of the hierarchy.

Nesting hierarchy is the parent hierarchy that has both advantages and disadvantages. The question for the designer, if they have to choose between one or the other of the solutions, is that concerning the required level of genericity: What is fixed? What is dynamic? For our part, we have chosen to implement both strategies in order to treat all types of ecosystems.

5.2.1.6. *The law of excluded middle*

The last essential point that we want to emphasize is the need to link ecosystem modeling data with an individual responsible for this modeling. In other words, what we are looking for in data management is the ability to include a third party, mainly because from an ethical and scientific point of view it seems fundamental to not dissociate this modeling information from the actor who produced them. We advocate an approach that aims to express an interpretation rather than the definition of a truth.

In concrete terms, to achieve this inclusion of the third party, we associate the actor who is the creator of each relationship between the existential dimensions of the ecosystem. Whether it is the work of an algorithm, a historical actor or a user of the ecosystem, it is possible to know who the modellers are, and thus, integrate a critique on the point of view that they express. Moreover, this categorization of data in terms of the actor offers the possibility of calculating contact recommendations between actors according to similarities or differences in their modeling approaches.

We define the recommendation by a matrix that relates the four existential dimensions of the ecosystem by weighting them positively according to the number of similarities and negatively according to the number of differences, the absence of a report corresponding to a weighting 0. For the calculation of similarities, we add the number of elements of each dimension with the same unique identifier for two different actors. For the calculation of the differences, we start from the similarities and add the elements of each dimension that are present in the modeling of one of the actors and not in the other. The resulting matrix is represented on a color scale to explore what makes actors more similar or more different.

5.2.2. Algorithmic platform to manage the ecosystem

Web platforms establish a client–server architecture by organizing communications with a server that responds to requests from multiple clients. These platforms operate on the basis of three technologies: a web server, a database server and a programming language. These three components are best known through the acronym AMP (Apache, MySql and PHP) that present them in their relationship with a LAMP operating system for Linux, XAMP for Windows and MAMP for Mac. Even if other client–server architectures exist, notably in Microsoft (IIS, SQL Server, .Net) or Java (Tomcat, Oracle, Java) universes, Apache technologies are dominant[42] due to their reliability, their "Open Source" licenses and the fact that they are free. These technologies make information flows available by opening

---

42 Even if the current trends show an increase in the power of Nginx: https://www.developpez.com/actu/129511/Serveurs-Web-Nginx-detient-desormais-un-tiers-des-parts-de-marche-tandis-qu-Apache-chute-en-dessous-des-50-pourcent- d-after-W3Tech /

access to digital resources via the "HTTP" communication protocol or "HTTPS" for the secure version. These resources are static, for example, in the case of an image file or dynamic when the resource being accessed is a program; this is the case, for example, of "PHP[43]" pages that execute an algorithm on the server before sending the information stream to the client who requested it.

We will not go into detail about the operation of an Apache web server, since many explanations are already available[44] and given the fact that this is not the purpose of this book. We will simply show in a diagram (Figure 5.12) how information flows between a user and a web server.

In the previous chapter, we presented our principles with regard to the database (see section 5.2.1). Let us now examine in more detail the algorithmic core of our platform by first presenting the PHP framework that we use, followed by the PHP libraries that we have put in place to control the knowledge ecosystem.

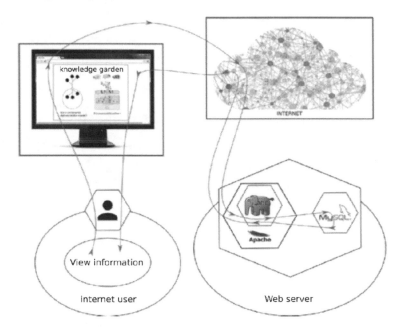

Figure 5.12. *Flow between a user and a web server*

---

43 See the documentation: https://secure.php.net/manual/en/intro-whatis.php
44 For example: https://apache.developpez.com/cours/

5.2.2.1. *Zend Framework*

In order to facilitate developments using computer objects that automate the management of information flows and to make these developments more accessible, understandable and maintainable through a community of coders, we have chosen to use a PHP framework. There are many[45], each with its own qualities and disadvantages. We chose the "Zend Framework" because it was developed by the creators of PHP and is therefore considered as the institutional framework of this language. In addition, it offers development tools as well as free and open source debugging[46]. Finally, it offers many applications such as code generators that automatically build the objects needed to drive a database[47], among others.

The organization of developments with the Zend Framework is based on the MVC model (Model–View–Controller) that we discussed in the introduction to this section (see section 5.2). For a Web application, the rules for the use of this framework impose a strict tree structure and the naming of particular files. By following these rules, developments gain in speed and reliability.

Today, the Knowledge Garden is made up of 40 or so controllers each with one or more views. We do not go into a detailed description of each of these controllers nor each of their views. Simply put, we organized these controllers into two categories: Tools and Projects. "Tool" controllers are used to manage generic information flows related to a particular technology or type of treatment. For example, the "graph" controller is used to generate data and display them according to different models of graphs, such as axes, radars, multiple lines, etc. Similarly, the "flow" controller is used to transmit information flows from sources such as DBpedia, Google Knowledge Graph, BNF data, etc. "Project" controllers are used to manage the information flows and user interfaces of Web applications developed in the context of research projects, such as the ANR Biolographes (see section C.1.1) and Aliento [SZO 15], or internal projects in the Paragraphe laboratory, such as the socio-semantic categorization of Gilles Deleuze's courses [SZO 15], the GAPAII project [HAC 12] or the ExCode HumaNum project (see section C.1.3).

---

45 For example: https://fr.wikipedia.org/wiki/Liste_de_frameworks_PHP
46 For example: https://eclipse.org/pdt/
47 For example: http://janitrix.developpez.com/zenerator/

Concerning the "models" layer of our Zend application, this one is organized in different domains corresponding to the database used by the platform. The platform primarily uses the "flow" database whose uses we have detailed in section 5.2.1. We used the Zend Framework principles to automate database management by creating a specific class for each table in the database. These classes are built with a model for property and methods that allowed us to automatically generate these classes and adapt them to the needs of each table. Note that in the platform we have put into effect multi-base management so that we can switch very easily from one database to another without having to modify the computer code. Therefore, we populated dozens of databases corresponding to particular projects but still maintain the interoperability of them all.

5.2.2.2. *Other PHP libraries*

In addition to the Zend Framework PHP classes and those we developed as part of the Zend MVC application, we created independent classes, and used classes created by other developers. These are essentially classes from the development kit provided by Google to manipulate its technological ecosystem[48]. We also use other classes that are useful for authentication management (CAS), the manipulation of RDF files (EasyRdf), the generation of Epub (Epub), etc. Regarding the independent PHP classes that we have developed, these are organized into five categories: API, Linked Open Data, Tools, Project and Scraping.

"API" type classes are used to manage information flows from APIs (see section 5.1.2.3) from several data providers such as Diigo, Flickr, Freebase, Google, HAL, ISTEX, Zotero, etc.[49] These classes retrieve the information from these suppliers and, if necessary, are able to store them so as to facilitate subsequent processing. For example, in the case of Diigo where the class dedicated to this API can store the data of users in order to save this information, or in the case of several people, compare their activities.

---

48 https://github.com/google/google-api-php-client
49 Complete list: http://gapai.univ-paris8.fr/jdc/phpDoc/packages/library.Flux.API.html

Linked Open Data classes[50] are used to consolidate data to make them interoperable with the global open data linking ecosystem (see section 5.1.2.5). For example, classes such as Flux_Databnf or Flux_DBpedia allow you to retrieve permanent references for documents or concepts, whereas the Flux_TEI or Flux_Skos classes allow you to manipulate data in these specific formats.

The "Tools" classes[51] are used for cross-cutting actions for all ecosystems. For example, the class "Flux_MC" allows us to manage the key words of the data by generating them from an algorithm, storing them or interrogating them. Another example is the class "Flux_Stats" which, as its name indicates, is used to make statistical treatments.

The "Project" classes have been developed so as not to overload the controllers with heavy and specific treatments for each project. For example, the class "Flux_EditInflu" contains algorithms for importing user data or complex queries for handling data and their renderings.

The "Scraping" classes are dedicated to recovering data from web pages that are analyzed with the goal of extracting structured information. For example, the class "Flux_Bup8" is used to obtain information about the works in a library without having to "negotiate" access to the IT services of this institution. While this practice is far less efficient and elegant than the internal deployment of an application within the information system, it provides flexibility for developments and the ability to quickly test multiple solutions without impacting IT. In addition, the projects developed in full transparency serve as arguments to contact the institution and make them a partner, and in so doing, thus make the prototype project evolve into a more complex operational application. The ExCode HumaNum project[52] perfectly illustrates this type of evolution (see section C.1.3).

5.2.3. *Editorial platform for controlling collaborative practices*

It is entirely possible to create your own platform to control the collaborative editing of information; however, development and maintenance costs are often too great when considering this type of solution. Since

---

50 List : http://gapai.univ-paris8.fr/jdc/phpDoc/packages/library.Flux.LinkedOpenData.html
51 List : http://gapai.univ-paris8.fr/jdc/phpDoc/packages/library.Flux.Outils.html
52 http://www.labex-arts-h2h.fr/excode-humanum.html

the advent of Web 2.0, information ecosystems have made collaborative publishing methods available to the public, accessed through simple tools: CMS (see section 5.1.2.9). In the Knowledge Garden, we use CMS SPIP, because it offers generic tools for collaborative publishing, the efficient management of multilingual content and the very fine-tuning of information flows.

5.2.3.1. *Common tools for collective publishing*

Collaborative tools are exceedingly numerous and offer a lot of very useful functions. We will not list an exhaustive inventory of these tools[53], but instead we will simply present those that we think are the most important ones that should be integrated into an information ecosystem.

The very first function is to create a network of people who will take part in the editorial work. To do this, it is necessary to make available to the public: registration forms, keyword recovery and editorial rules to give each person specific rights. These rules in turn make it possible to set up an editorial management, that is, the possibility (or not) of proposing content and submitting it to a committee, who will validate (or not) the publication of this content. The content will take the form of articles, comments, documents and even in some cases will give contributors the possibility to organize these contents so as to facilitate their discovery through effective site navigation.

Content organization generally follows two complementary strategies. The first is to create trees that, like taxonomies, will specify at each level of the tree how that particular branch is different to the previous branch(es). This is a strategy that Bruno Bachimont calls "differential semantics" as it is organized according to the relative position of a node with respect to two axes, that of the father and the brother in a tree:

"The meaning of a node is determined by its closest neighbors. In a tree, the closest neighbors are on the one hand the parent unit and on the other hand the sister units. It is therefore necessary to determine the meaning of a node according to its parent and its brothers." [BAC 07, p. 142]

---

53 For a functional analysis grid of CMS, visit: http://www.cmsmatrix.org/

In addition to this very useful strategy for hierarchical identification, a strategy aimed at creating transversal relationships between the thematic branches through key words should not be neglected. We note that it is also possible to create keyword hierarchies to create a multidimensional semantic grid. Examples of semantic grids are becoming increasingly common in faceted search engines [DES 13] in order to build browsing potential where user responsibility in content selection is far more important than in a unique tree strategy.

For collective content publishing, an important feature is the tools for the easy deployment of display templates. We will deal with these objects in greater detail further on (see section 5.2.4.1.1), but at this stage we would like to emphasize the ability of CMS to easily integrate these templates into their operation. Regarding SPIP, the integration of graphic templates is facilitated by the provision of a simplified syntax for users to display the contents being created in the "back-office". The SPIP "loops"[54] are indeed a simple way to make database queries without having to know the SQL language. Moreover, in this CMS, a large number of "tags"[55] make it possible to easily display registration forms or to leave comments.

To conclude this quick presentation on the most useful tools for collaborative publishing, let us mention the "plugins" that offer the possibility of extending the functionality of a CMS through the addition of extra modules. In the case of SPIP, these plugins are numerous[56] and can be easily installed from repositories that host and evaluate the relevance of the proposed features.

5.2.3.2. *Multilingual content management*

Among the uses of CMS, the management of multilingualism is undoubtedly one of the most useful. Indeed, the internationalization of audiences brought together through the Web requires support for several languages in order to make the content distributed by a website accessible to different language speakers. SPIP is particularly effective at internationalizing content by using plugins that make it easier to manage multilingualism.

---

54 http://www.spip.net/fr_article898.html
55 http://www.spip.net/fr_article1902.html
56 http://plugins.spip.net/

We have seen that in the Knowledge Garden, a Zend application manages the algorithmic processing of information flows (see section 5.2.2.1), but in order to manage the multilingual dimension, SPIP provides tools that are directly operational and easy to use. For example, we used these tools to translate the screens of the prototype we are developing to map knowledge (see section C.1.2).

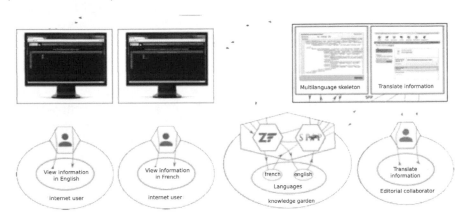

Figure 5.13. *Publishing management of translation flows*

The diagram in Figure 5.13 shows how the coupling of SPIP and Zend differentiates editing work for content translation and information flow management for the display of multilingual data. For example, in the emotion categorization tool, we developed a "wheel of emotions"[57] view in the "graph" controller. This controller manages the reading and writing of an information flow; however, in order to manage several languages, it is far easier to go use one of the SPIP internationalization tools.

5.2.3.3. *Information flow settings*

The development of an editorial platform to manage the flow of information in a knowledge ecosystem requires a continual negotiation between a desire to make these developments generic and the need to make them easily understandable, usable and maintainable. The designers and coders of this platform are faced with a dilemma between generic and "hard" settings.

---

57 Diagram: http://gapai.univ-paris8.fr/jdc/public/graph/roueemotion; source code: https://github.com/samszo/jardindesconnaissances/blob/master/application/views/scripts/graph/rouee motion.phtml

Generic coders have the ambition to write algorithms that can adapt to the maximum types of situations with a minimum of codes; they are looking for an elegant and transparent code to describe the algorithm. In order to adapt to situations, the algorithms take into account the variables that characterize these situations through a setting, which is sometimes very complex and as a result very precise. The Gephi network template software perfectly illustrates this point since the genericity of a networked representation composed of only three dimensions (node, link and anchor) is counterbalanced by placement algorithms, the settings for which will elude most users who will fumble until they obtain a result that will reinforce their preconceived idea.

Conversely, "hard" or specific developments integrate the settings of the algorithm directly into its coding. This type of platform targets specific purposes and uses, they cannot adapt, they are very stable black boxes, very easily maintainable and usable. The user has only the minimum of choices to make, or even none at all other than triggering the algorithm. The most glaring example of this type of platform is probably Facebook, which offers minimal interaction to the user who clicks on a "like" button and leaves it up to the algorithm to calculate the consequences of this choice.

Between the two approaches, there is no question of choosing since it brings both advantages and disadvantages. In the end, it will be the user experiences that will make the platforms evolve towards a more generic and therefore more complex system setting, or towards a simpler but more limited hard setting. We note that Linked Open Data proposals tend towards an ever greater genericity given that the formalisms that are recommended have the goal of smoother setting parameters and to achieve an interoperability and transparency of the algorithms through the use of ontological variables. What is at stake is the capacity of knowledge ecosystems to take into account hypercomplex configurations in the form of existences modeled according to ontological norms such as OWL. Therefore, the most fascinating challenge is the accessing of the largest number of these ontological models, and thus human–machine interfaces, which in turn will facilitate these setting parameters.

5.2.4. *Client applications to explore ecosystem views*

We have just seen the models that manage the data (see section 5.2.1), and the controllers which deal with the computation and algorithmic dimension (see section 5.2.2). Now, let us look at the third set of elements that make up an MVC architecture: the views. These are the graphical interfaces through which users access data through algorithms. We conceive of them as map layers, accessible for reading and writing (see section 4.2). They serve as means with which to explore a knowledge ecosystem with the dual purpose of the map for the explorer: to go into space in order to explore it, to formalize the exploration pathways.

In this chapter, we will describe the technical aspects of these cartographic interfaces by first presenting the principles of graphic design that we used to develop the Knowledge Garden platform. In a second step, we will detail the principles for the interactions between the views and the controllers, concluding with the main computer coding technologies that we use.

5.2.4.1. *Graphic design*

The first point we would like to emphasize is the graphic design of the views. We will not focus here on the aesthetic aspects, but rather we will focus on a design method by "model" or "template" which today seems to us the most practical. We will then propose another more experimental method based on screens drawn using Scalable Vector Graphics (or SVG).

5.2.4.1.1. The graphical models

Today, we find on the Web a multitude of templates[58] that bid to design a website, with turnkey solutions downloadable for free or for a few tens of euros. These templates are composed from the three basic languages for Web design: HTML, CSS and JavaScript. They save a lot of time in the development of a website, since we can simply use the template directly or make adaptations without having to master all the technologies used. On the contrary, they offer a good starting point for those who want to learn more about these technologies, by working from concrete examples that they can modify little by little in order to better discern the technical subtleties.

---

58 Some links to examples: https://www.diigo.com/user/luckysemiosis?query=templates

Figure 5.14. *Two implementations of the same graphical template*

The important points to consider when choosing a template are:

– ease of use: templates must be functional as soon as they are downloaded. A simple display and navigation test validates this point;

– adaptation to the format: we say that the template is "responsive" when it is able to automatically adapt to different screen sizes: desktop, tablet, mobile, etc.

Compliance with standards: it is important that the template conforms to W3C-defined Web standards[59].

By facilitating the development of websites, the templates tend to impose a particular aspect for the pages. This trend is all the more important since graphic templates are recommended by key online players. Google, for example, has been offering graphic and design rules for websites and mobile applications since 2014: Material Design[60]. These recommendations provide all the vocabulary needed to build graphical interfaces that tend to become interaction standards, such as the trigram ≡ which signifies the location of a menu that can be expanded.

Even if these templates are adaptable and independent of the content that will be displayed, we still wonder whether this desire to homogenize this aspect of the Web comes at the expense of graphic diversity and decreases the accessibility of information. On the contrary, it encourages creativity and open mindedness.

5.2.4.1.2. SVG HMIs

Another more experimental web design approach is to draw Human–Machine Interfaces (HMIs) in SVG (Scalable Vector Graphics[61]) with a vector-based modeling tool like Illustrator[62] or its freeware equivalent: Inkscape[63]. This method aims to overcome the graphic limitations of HTML, making web design more accessible to graphic designers, and to optimize the dynamism of pages and their interactivities.

Inspired by the layout principles inherited from print, HTML works with rectangular blocks that take the graphic codes of the press page and do not involve irregular compositions. For example, it is extremely difficult, if not impossible, to create curves, entanglements or star graphic blocks in HTML, like the "wheel of emotions" presented in Figure 5.15.

---

59 Link to the W3C validation engine: https://validator.w3.org/
60 Link to the website: https://material.io/
61 Link to the official website: https://www.w3.org/Graphics/SVG/
62 Link to the software: http://www.adobe.com/products/illustrator.html
63 Link to the software: https://inkscape.org

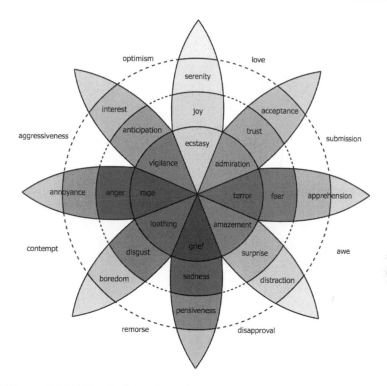

Figure 5.15. *Wheel of emotions. For a color version of the figure, see
www.iste.co.uk/szoniecky/ecosystems.zip*

Thanks to SVG vector drawing, it is quite possible to model the irregular
blocks composing the star in Figure 5.15, or even more complex graphical
structures without being limited by HTML. Above all, these models are
carried out with the pallets of tools dedicated to drawing (Bezier curves,
polygons, stars, gradients, etc.[64]), which makes their creation much easier,
becoming accessible to graphic designers who have not mastered HTML.
Indeed, the creation of interfaces in SVG eliminates the integration work that
it is now necessary to do in order to adapt the design concepts proposed by
graphic artists in the form of images into the HTML format. By using SVG,
these images become directly usable in a Web environment without having
to translate them into HTML.

---

64 For a complete list of drawing tools available in the Inkscape software, see: http://write.
flossmanuals.net/inkscape/about-inkscape/

What is particularly interesting in the SVG format is the ability to compose or decompose graphic elements in order to make them dynamic and interactive. In SVG, just like in HTML, each graphic element is defined by an XML tag which specifies the type of element (element group, circle, rectangle, curves, text, etc.) and the attributes of these elements (sizes, colors, positions, etc.). Among the attributes available, there is one that is particularly interesting, the one that defines for each graphic element a unique identifier (Illustrator and Inkscape do it automatically). The "id" attribute, while respecting the fundamental principle of the uniqueness of information, makes it possible to transform a drawing into a relational database (see section 5.1.3.6). Therefore, it is possible to perform on the graphical elements the basic operations of information manipulation (see section 5.1.3) so as to dynamically evolve the interfaces according to the interaction scenarios. These are put in place by defining for the graphic elements the attributes dedicated to interactivity[65] so that they trigger an event on a click, a mouse hover, etc.

We will see in the following chapter how to technically implement these dynamics and interactions. At this stage, let us just emphasize that the graphic liberation brought about when SVG is coupled with a relational management of information flows for each graphic element tends to make Web HMIs autonomous existences evolving within knowledge ecosystems.

5.2.4.2. *Dynamic interaction methods*

We have just seen how the interfaces are transformed into autonomous, dynamic and interactive existences by the unique identification of the graphic elements and the addition of an interaction event. We will now examine how to manage these dynamics and interactions through JavaScript language[66]. We will first discuss the simple principles of dynamism and interactions with data via controllers, then we will review the JavaScript libraries that today seem essential to us for the development of a Web platform. Our goal is not to detail the development techniques or functions of the libraries, but rather to describe the basic methods for managing dynamic interactions.

---

65 Complete list of events: https://www.w3.org/TR/SVG11/script.html#EventAttributes
66 JavaScript language references: https://developer.mozilla.org/en/docs/Web/JavaScript

5.2.4.2.1. Interactions with data

In addition to the languages used to manage the graphical aspects of Web resources (HTML, SVG, CSS, etc.), JavaScript is a programming language used to manage dynamisms and interactions. To put it simply, JavaScript is the means of bringing static resources to life by determining the actions to take when events occur. The role of the coder is to program these actions and to predict when they will be triggered. The role of the graphic designer is to make visible the potentiality of these actions and their results. Consider, for example, the wheel of emotions presented in Figure 5.15 in order to explain how to manage the dynamics and interactions of this graph so as to collect a user's emotions and compile them in a database.

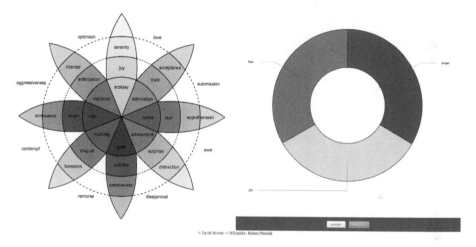

Figure 5.16. *HMI to harvest the emotions. For a color version of the figure, see www.iste.co.uk/szoniecky/ecosystems.zip*

This interface is composed of four parts: a title, a wheel of emotions on the left, a circular "donut" chart on the right, with the acknowledgments and references below. The purpose of this GUI is to collect the emotions of a user and store these emotions in a database and then analyze them. We chose a very simple interaction since the description of an emotion is done by simply clicking on one of the categories proposed by Robert Plutchik [PLU 91] to add a component of the emotion or to remove this component from the "donut". The recording of an emotion in the database is done when the user presses the "save" button.

To create these interactions, we have developed functions in JavaScript that have different purposes. Here are the details for two of them:

– add event listeners to the graphic elements. After having selected the texts (see below line 3) of the "wheel of emotions", the program "associates" data with this text (l.4) and "asks" it to react when the user clicks on it (l.6), stating that this reaction will be to increase the weight of this emotion (l.8) and to visualize the choice of emotions (l.10). This same function specifies that the pointer of the mouse will turn into a "+" icon when the mouse passes over it (l.13). All these purposes translate into a few lines of JavaScript code:

```
1.  Function ajoutEvent() {
2.      //ajoute l'écouteur d'événement sur les textes
3.      txts = d3.selectAll('text')
4.          .data(roueData)
5.          .attr('class','txtRoueEmo')
6.          .on('click',function(d, i){
7.              //augmente la valeur de l'émotion
8.              d.value ++;
9.              //affiche les modifications de choix
10.             changeChoix(roueData);
11.         });
12.     //ajoute un curseur + aux textes du graphique
13.     $('.txtRoueEmo').awesomeCursor('plus', {
14.         color: 'black',
15.         outline: 'red'
16.     });
17. }
```

– save the choice in the database. This generic feature is used to store information in the database and retrieve information about the registration process. The communication between the client application in JavaScript and the PHP controllers that will handle the transactions with the database uses an asynchronous method that allows for it to send a set of data to the server, and to continue the execution of the JavaScript code without having to wait for the answer. This method, historically known as AJAX (Asynchronous JavaScript and XML), has been transformed to replace XML with another language dedicated to the manipulation of data: JSON (see section 5.1.3.3). Here are the few lines of code needed to perform these transactions:

```
 1.  function saveRepQuest(dt) {
 2.      $.ajax({
 3.          URL: "saverepquest",
 4.          data: dt,
 5.          type: 'post',
 6.          dataType: 'json',
 7.          error: function(error){
 8.              try {
 9.                  var js = JSON.parse(error.responseText);
10.              } catch (e) {
11.                  w2alert("Erreur : "+e);
12.              }
13.          },
14.          success: function(result) {
15.              saveResult = result;
16.          }
17.      });
18.  }
```

These two examples of JavaScript function show how it is possible in a few lines to manage the interactions of a graph with a database. However, to achieve this simplicity, the codes we presented use JavaScript libraries that are very useful.

5.2.4.2.2. JavaScript libraries

It is difficult today to count the number of JavaScript libraries available on the Web or even the "frameworks" dedicated to this language. The collaborative development platform GitHub gives us an indication of this proliferation by counting, at the time of writing, more than 150,000 JavaScript projects led by more than four thousand developers (Figure 5.17). Many sites offer rankings of the most efficient or the most fashionable JavaScript technologies, but in the world of the Web, the constant and rapid evolution of uses coupled with a proliferation of developers makes it absolutely unavoidable to conduct personal and ongoing monitoring of these technologies so as to continually adapt their own practices. That said, today, two libraries seem unavoidable for the development of a Web application: jQuery and D3.js.

Figure 5.17. *JavaScript in GitHub*[67]

jQuery[68] is one of the historical JavaScript libraries. It was created in 2006 to meet the growing needs of developers who wanted to manipulate HTML pages more easily without having to reload the page completely. This is, for example, what we do in the function "*saveRepQuest*" that we presented above (see 1.2 *$.ajax*). The use of this library goes through a single character that includes all the features: "$". This economy of means is also put forward in the library's slogan: "write less, do more". The success of this technology can be measured by the thousands of extensions that use jQuery to develop new features. For example, in the "addEvent" function (see 113 *.awesomeCursor* above), we use a jQuery extension that allows us to draw from a library of icons the mouse cursors[69].

D3[70] is a JavaScript library created by Stanford researchers [BOS 11] to help developers create dynamic, interactive and data-driven graphs. D3 or D^3 stands for "Data Driven Document", where the challenge is to build documents driven by data by associating value tables with graphic forms. We find in this ambition the manipulation principles for the creation of interactions from data flows presented by [CAR 99]:

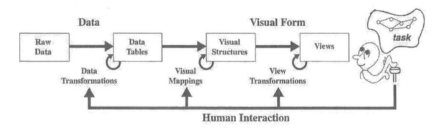

Figure 5.18. *Graphics modeling flow [CAR 99]*

---

67 Link to the current figures: https://github.com/search?l=JavaScript&Q=javascript
68 Link to the official website: http://jquery.com/
69 Link to extension: https://github.com/jwarby/jquery-awesome-cursor
70 Link to the official site: https://d3js.org/

Like jQuery, D3 is now used by other libraries as a basis for the development of new features, for web applications, or to simplify the development of graphics by proposing more easily configurable templates[71]. The collection of available examples[72] also shows the success of this technology, which requires a significant investment in order to understand the principles of selection and association of data, but quickly becomes profitable through the opportunities that it offers. For example, here is how in a line of code, it is possible to create a color scale that transforms a value between 1 and 100 into its red and blue equivalents:

```
var color = d3.scaleLinear()
    .domain([1, 100])
    .range(["red", "blue"]);
```

We could multiply the library or JavaScript framework examples to show the diversity of the available functionalities, for example, to manage geographical dimensions (Google Map[73], Leaflet[74], etc.), to model universes in three dimensions (Three.js[75]), to manage forms and spreadsheets (W2ui.js[76]) and manipulate videos (amalia.js[77], popcorn.js[78]). However, our purpose here was not to detail all these technologies, but simply to show that JavaScript has become an essential language in the developing of dynamisms and interactions.

5.2.5. From technical specification to the organization of collective intelligence

The panorama which we have just described in order to specify what is a Web platform for the development of knowledge ecosystems, has led us from the general principles of the resources available on the Web, to the very technical details needed to develop this type of platform according to an MVC model. These considerations give an idea of the project that such a work represents, but in order to be complete, we must now speak of a

---

71 Here are two examples: http://www.highcharts.com/ and http://dimplejs.org/
72 Link to the example page: https://github.com/d3/d3/wiki/Gallery
73 https://developers.google.com/maps
74 http://leafletjs.com/
75 https://threejs.org/
76 http://w2ui.com/web/
77 https://ina-foss.github.io/amalia.js/
78 http://mozilla.github.io/popcorn-docs/getting-started/

fundamental dimension that goes beyond the technical, that which affects the use of these technologies and the organization of the collective intelligence needed to make these uses productive for everyone.

Using the diagram presented in Figure 5.18 [CAR 99] to explain the different steps and feedback loops through which information flows are used to transform raw data into dynamic and interactive graphs, we realize that an important step is missing in order for our approach to be complete: that of the production of raw data by the knowledge ecosystems themselves. We believe that the [CAR 99] model needs to be enriched by a new feedback loop that will validate the production of data through a collective intelligence process and which will aim to assess the ethical dimensions of these data. Therefore, we propose an updated model that takes into account these additions:

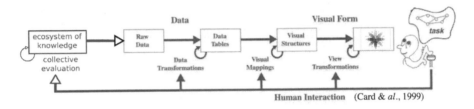

Figure 5.19. *Modeling from knowledge ecosystems. For a color version of the figure, see www.iste.co.uk/szoniecky/ecosystems.zip*

Raw data is produced by knowledge ecosystems and then modeled to provide users with interfaces that will be used to collectively validate the ecosystems that will produce new data and so on, until a task is finalized, or in a process without end, in the manner of a work in progress. The organization of this reflexive cycle raises many questions that we have already discussed (see sections 5.1.1 and 4.1). More generally, the biggest problem associated with this type of project lies in the ability of individuals to organize and manage collectively these reflexive flows which, for the moment, are mainly in GAFAM tools, a little in the laws of governments and soon perhaps controlled by crowds of anonymous people. It is important that we are aware of the dangers generated by these reflexive processes, especially if we consider that each child will be able throughout his schooling to build an extremely precise representation on all of their learning and their experiences [SZO 14b]. Do we not need a public service ensuring the conservation and ethical valorisation of these Knowledge Gardens?

Conclusion

And, once again,
it is up to us to rediscover
a way of being a Being
- before, after, here and everywhere else -,
without however being identical to itself;
a processual, polyphonic Being
singularizable by infinitely complexifiable textures,
according to the infinite speeds which animate
its virtual compositions
Félix Guattari[1]

Thus it may be said that a Monad
can only come into being or
come to an end all at once; that is to say,
it can come into being only by creation
and come to an end only by annihilation,
while that which is compound
comes into being or comes to an end by parts.
TG. W. Leibniz[2]

Through this book, we hope that we have shown the importance of the notion of the ecosystem and how its application in the field of knowledge management opens up interesting avenues for research and development perspectives for intelligent technologies.

1 Translation of quote from http://limen.mi2.hr/limen1-2001/stephen_arnott.html.
2 Translation of quote from https://www.plato-philosophy.org/wp-content/uploads/2016/07/The-Monadology-1714-by-Gottfried-Wilhelm-LEIBNIZ-1646-1716.pdf.

The work we have presented here reflects only a part of the research we have conducted to develop a collective intelligence platform for the development of knowledge ecosystems. Above all, they mark the boundary of the research still to be carried out, in particular, to validate the design principles that we adopt and to find new ones. This work, which remains to be done, is shared between the field of experimentation and that of theoretical research.

C.1. Experiments: digital humanities and e-Education

Although the Knowledge Garden is only a prototype, it has allowed us to experience its relevant use in the fields of digital humanities and E-education. For example, here are research projects in the making that use the principles we have presented in this book.

C.1.1. *Mapping the networks of influence3*

The question of influence is at the heart of all research in the human and social sciences that question the relationships between people, events, objects and the consequences of their interactions. At the onset of digital research tools, it is becoming increasingly necessary to formalize this research so as to make them interoperable with initiatives around Linked Open Data (see section 5.1.2.5). The objective is to be able to limit the problems of ambiguity in the scientific discourse by categorizing the objects of research with perennial references. For example, does an analysis of "Victor Hugo" refer to the famous French writer born in 1802 or to the Spanish salsa singer who died in 1960? If a researcher is interested in the singer, their information sources will be extremely polluted by information on the writer that inevitably arrives from a query with the character chain "Victor Hugo". A simple way to solve this problem is to categorize the string with a unique identifier such as the International Standard Name Identifier (ISNI). Thus, Victor Hugo, the writer, is defined by "0000 0001 2 120 098" and Victor Hugo, the singer, by "0000 0000 0100 2666".

To facilitate this work of categorization, we have developed a prototype that allows us to find references from a string search and then choose the answer that corresponds to what the researcher wishes to designate. We offer four different formulas in order to find references of people, documents, places and concepts. Here, for example, Figure C.1 shows an interface that allows us to find a document.

---

3 This research is presented in detail here [SAO 17b].

From these references of actors, documents, concepts and places, a graphical interface will make it possible to map the relations between these various elements and to categorize their relations. For example, a researcher can create a network of influence networks between a scientist and his students, between an artist and his inspirers, etc. The map can then be used as a basis for calculating contact recommendations with other researchers who are working on the same topics, or reading relevant documents.

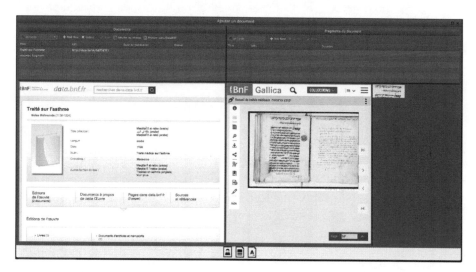

Figure C.1. *Formula for the search of documentary references*

C.1.2. *Mapping wisdoms*[4]

The objective of this research project is to model and map the interpretations of proverbs by people around the world. We seek to evaluate the degree of analogical proximity for proverbial expressions through this work:

> "To what degree of generality does a proverb apply? What is the extent of the situations to which a proverb can be attributed without this being exaggerated or even incongruous? [...] Finally, where are the categorical boundaries defined implicitly by our proverb?" [HOF 13, p. 134]

4 This research takes place in the framework of a workshop CreaTIC laboratory (http:// gapai.univ-paris8.fr/CreaTIC/E-education/Proverbes/) and in collaboration with researchers in the ANR project Aliento (http://aliento.msh-lorraine.fr/).

At the same time, we wish to question the hypothesis that there are "semantic *terroir*" particular to specific geographical areas in order to better manage the difficulties inherent to the interculturality of knowledge engineering projects:

> "The diversity of models and theasaurusi grouped together and proposed in open access on the LOD [Linked Open Data] community platform testifies to the cultural need to adapt conceptual models to the professional, national or local contexts of organizations. It also shows that the current difficulties in implementing LOD are not due to technical obstacles, but to different cultural visions within the Semantic Web ecosystem" [JUA 16, section 27].

As part of a collective interpretation game [LÉV 11, p. 319] whose purpose is to make players aware of the ecology of attention and the importance of a reflexive approach, the application "mapping wisdoms" proposes the forms of wisdom to a user that they must interpret from formulas that use cartographic principles (see section 4.2). For now, the application offers only texts, although we plan to submit users, images, movies and sounds to wisdom.

The texts we propose come from an automatic proverb generator that we developed in light of the work by Jean-Pierre Balpe.[5] With each interrogation, the generator displays a text by choosing from a corpus of proverbs retrieved from websites or by automatically generating a text with generative formulas constructed from true proverbs. For example, the formula "[proverb-A good X good Y]" built from the French proverb "To a good cat, a good rat" allows one to generate new proverbs by replacing the words "good", "cat" and "rat" by other adjectives, other predatory animals and other prey animals.[6]

The goal is to confront the user with false proverbs so as to evaluate their ability to discern those which seem right to them. In addition to the interest in learning languages, this device is very useful for analyzing primitive analogies [HOF 13] at the root of many proverbs. Our hypothesis is that these analogies are the path of a popular wisdom related to that particular territory. By collecting multiple interpretations of these proverbs in different

---

5 http://www.balpe.name/
6 http://gapai.univ-paris8.fr/gen/services/api.php?oeu=57&cpt=169965&nb=1

parts of the world, we think that we can map the use and nonuse of these analogies in order to define sapiential borders or, on the contrary, universal forms of knowledge.

C.1.3. *Exploring the sources of knowledge*

Similar to the project above, we are also working to design, develop and test a "collective interpretation game", but this time, our field of experimentation is that of the exploration of knowledge. Inspired by the board game Tantrix, we create a Web platform and a smartphone game whose goal is to organize the individual and collective exploration for a given knowledge source (libraries, archives, museums, conferences, etc.).

Figure C.2. *Tantrix board game*

The goal of the game is to link documents with themes. The documents are referenced in a semantic map on which players will place tiles with colored lines corresponding to that of their team. The goal is to build the longest line so as to map a maximum number of relations between documents. Each tile may be subject to a controversy that will result in a debate and subsequent vote. In addition to the fact that this game makes it possible to learn the operation of a knowledge source through its mapping, it also gives the means to create a network of expertise between people who respond to questionnaires.

The game we propose is placed in the field of "serious games" [DUP 11, LAF 15], which in recent years has been developing both in the field of continuing education and in the field of basic research. With the rules it proposes, the game creates a potential for action by framing the player's actions in a system of constraints that is reminiscent of the creative processes invented by the *oulipians* [BLO 14].

We borrow our constraint system from an existing strategy game: Tantrix (Figure C.2). This choice is motivated by the analogy between the purpose of this game and one of the fundamental principles of intellectual work: to connect [MOR 99]. Moreover, as a puzzle that relates a grid-like plateau with elements that draw a line, Tantrix shares a commonality with another analogy, that of weaving [MUG 06]. Ultimately, Tantrix allows one to put collective strategies into place that do not only aim to beat opponents by generating the longest line in a single color but also collaborate with other teams to build the greatest number of links, whatever the color.

Figure C.3. *A screenshot of ExplAgora*

By transposing the Tantrix rules into intellectual work, we want to develop a process for the collective categorization of knowledge [BRO 11, LAT 12] that is independent from the information source and simple enough to be accessible to as many people as possible. The direction gleaned from this strategy game seems a good way to graphically organize the intellectual work so as to make the understanding of the rules for participation more accessible to us. The difficulties encountered on the AIME platform (see http://modesofexistence.org/) show that it is not so easy to understand how a collective process works, even when motivated to do so. The playful principle of progression through the levels allows one to accompany the player in the understanding of the game, by guiding them from the simplest steps (find a document, to associate a theme, etc.), to the most complex ones (to model a document grid, to propose a thesaurus, etc.).

Through this project, we want to evaluate to what extent our models are relevant and accessible and how a game of collective intelligence gives cultural institutions an opportunity to occupy a privileged niche in the ecology of attention. In partnership with ergonomists, the project is based on an empirical analysis of the activities considered for this application, namely the individual and collective exploration of documentary collections. It's about understanding what are the issues and needs related to this activity and to see how the developed application transforms this activity.

C.2. Theoretical fields to whet the appetite

At the end of this book, many questions were not addressed, as well as certain key concepts and authors prominent in the field of knowledge ecosystems. The following lines are intended to define perspectives for theoretical research and to awaken the reader's curiosity toward aspects of our problem that we have not yet had the opportunity to deal with.

C.2.1. *Guattari's ecosophy*

The first great absentee of this book is without doubt Felix Guattari whose thought infuses this work even if we have not yet quoted it. It would take a whole chapter to present his tripartition of the ecology between environmental, social and mental practices [GUA 89a] and show how it fits with the modeling principles that we defend. Similarly, regarding the importance of mapping practice, which must never neglect the critical dimension:

"all systems for defining models are in a sense equal, all are tenable, but only to the extent that their principles of intelligibility renounce any universalist pretensions, and that their sole mission be to help map real existing territories (sensory, cognitive, affective and aesthetic universes) - and even then only in relation to carefully delimited areas and periods"[7] [GUA 89b, p. 10].

Finally, Guattari's contribution should also be explored in his analysis of subjectivities and the way machines interfere with them in order to transform their uses and assist in the construction of new existential universes:

"The chaosmic fold of deterritorialisation and the autopoietic fold of enunciation, with their interface of existential grasping and transmonadism, implant at the heart of the object-subject relation - and before any instance of representation - a creative processuality, an ontological responsibility which binds liberty and its ethical vertigo at the heart of ecosystemic necessities"[8] [GUA 92, p. 174].

C.2.2. *Semiotic principles of the µ group*

The other great absentees of this book which we will have to explore and integrate into our reflections are the semiotic principles of the µ group. For more than 50 years, this research group has been asking the fundamental question: why is there meaning rather than nothing?

These researchers adopted a methodological attitude that aims at an ambition of generality and a concern for economy, which allowed them to propose a very small number of concepts, take, for example, their last work where there are only two: "dipole" and "duality" [GRO 15]. These are the concepts that we would like to evaluate in view of our proposals, especially in connection with "semiotic life cycle". As such, we would like to find new design principles and participate in the movement initiated by this group:

---

7 Translation of quote from https://monoskop.org/images/4/4b/Genosko_Gary_ed_The_Guattari_Reader.pdf.
8 Translation of quote from https://monoskop.org/images/2/24/Guattari_Felix_Chaosmosis_An_Ethico-Aesthetic_Paradigm.pdf.

"The opportunity that is offered today to the science of meaning is to join the experimental currents, not only to save oneself, but to fertilize them, by offering rigorously founded concepts, which will manifest with them their heuristic value"[9] [GRO 15, p. 531].

C.2.3. *The power to act and activity analysis*

In this book, we have repeatedly approached the concept of the power to act by putting it at the heart of the ethical question, understood as the choice by a collective or individual actor to increase or decrease his power so as to act in a specific context and for a definite purpose. It will probably be necessary to clarify this definition through a recent work in activity analysis and see if the principles we propose are in line with the concerns of researchers such as Gaspard Brun. In particular, we are specifically interested in this author's [BRU 17] analyses of Yves Clot's work [CLO 08], which compares the power to act, activity analysis and Spinoza's philosophy.

C.2.4. *Political ecology*

Political ecology is a theme that has not been mentioned in this book even though it is of fundamental importance, particularly given the fact that this area of thought is the bearer of many initiatives and the source of very stimulating reflections, as evidenced by the journal *Multitudes.*[10] We think particularly of the works of Yann Moulier-Boutang whose economic and political thought is fed by the analogy of the garden:

"The seeds are dispersed in the wind, the rains water the lands, the bees pollinate the fields according to dynamics very different from those which govern business practices. It is, among other things, reintegrating our modes of production and consumption into these more general ecological dynamics that we will afford ourselves the chance to overcome the current deadends of the dominant restricted economism"[11] [MOU 06, section 30].

---

9 Translation of French quote.
10 http://www.cairn.info/revue-multitudes.htm
11 Translation of French quote.

Beyond this analogical proximity, this research provides avenues for reflection on the societal challenges of intellectual technologies, particularly in relation to the question on the ecology of attention that we have discussed without analyzing the political and economic consequences thereof:

> "An unconditional income of existence is the essential condition for the recognition of the ecology of attention that we need in order to face the challenges of the future"[12] [CIT 16, section 34].

C.2.5. *Personal learning environments*

The last area we would like to point out as a research topic still in need of exploration is the personal learning environments (or PLEs) [HEN 14]. In view of our ambition to develop a collective intelligence platform in order to cultivate knowledge, it is essential to accurately analyze how PLE researchers provide operational frameworks for the design and methodology of critical evaluation.

C.3. Scientific practices between calculable facts and sensible intuition

Is it always possible to explain why the gesture takes one direction rather than another? In an internal reflexivity deeper than that of a calculable logic, the intuitive gestures express a position whose clarity depends on the sensitivity of each actor. What does the brand of paint used on a particular work by Twombly matter to us?

As scientists, our role is to erase the inspiration provided by the esthetic experience so as to make the knowledge it generates shareable. The further away we are from the materiality of knowledge of the first kind, that which physical facts bring, the more the calculability of this knowledge dissolves, and hence the possibility of a comprehensive sharing of said knowledge. By plunging ourselves into the interiority of conceptual intuitions in order to express what seems right to us, we open up a sharing space wherein ideas illuminate like lightning bolts, and from which we can transmit only the emotional vibration that this energetic flow emerges. At this point,

---

12 Translation of French quote.

knowledge sharing is not about words but about sensitivity. At the frontier of the material exterior and the sensible interior, between these two infinities lie the plane of scientific discourse made up of logical relations between calculable facts and conceptual intuitions.

Inspired by philosophical, anthropological, sociological, biological, quantic and poetic works, we would like to open the field of computer design to other logic and coherences other than those of the engineering sciences. For example, we see in Gilles Deleuze a designer of thought, who invents the plans of intellectual technologies that are yet to be made. However, he is not the only one; many other thinkers have provided some of the earliest design perspectives, such as Epicurus, Paracelsus, Leibniz and as we have shown, Spinoza.

Let us hope that the scientific austerity of these pages contributes to their understanding and stimulates the curious to continue their experiments on knowledge ecosystems in a more sensitive manner.

Appendix

A.1. Project planning the new platform[1]

After years of development and testing, we are today at the stage where the Knowledge Garden is in need of a complete overhauling. In its current version, the Knowledge Garden is more of a prototype than a tool in the sense that only its designer masters its uses. We are challenged with an overgrown bramble, with multiple entanglements and snags of all kinds, rather than the contemplation of tidy perspectives afforded by, say, a French garden. The Knowledge Garden is a work in progress [ECO 79] whose manufacturing secrets are perfectly readable due to its availability through Open Source, but also perfectly opaque due to the complexity of the implementations. Here is undoubtedly one of the crucial problems of the relationship between Art and Science, that of the reproducibility of experience, or to put it another way, that of the complete explicitation of intuition.

The purpose of this appendix is to plan and budget the development of a new version of the Knowledge Garden by guiding this project towards the realization of a collective intelligence platform for the development of digital educational resources.

A.1.1. *Objectives*

To complete this Knowledge Garden redesign, we shall break this project down into five main sub-objectives.

---

1 This Appendix has been carried out in collaboration with Philippe Bootz.

A.1.1.1. *Monitoring science and technology*

This first objective aims to gather the most up-to-date information for six scientific and technological fields. This monitoring work will make it possible to specify in a reference document the conceptual and technical frameworks that will be used to develop the IT tools necessary for our objectives. Each area will lead to the publication of a report and ultimately to the drafting of the technical specifications of the project. A Diigo account will be created to archive and disseminate information collected on the Web. Similarly, regarding the bibliography, a Zotero account and group will be created.

A.1.1.1.1. Platform for archiving scientific data

Through this work, we hope to gather information to better specify how to manage the scientific archives. Special attention will be paid to issues of sustainability, interoperability, cost and confidentiality. This last point is particularly important for the collection of digital pathways that the pedagogical resources will generate.

A.1.1.1.2. Domain ontologies

Of the many ontologies developed under Linked Open Data (LOD), there are certainly some that are useful to this project. The purpose of this watch is to specify which ontologies can be used.

A.1.1.1.3. Interoperable languages for the human sciences

In addition to the ontologies that make it possible to define the conceptual bases of digital data, it is necessary to use languages that put these ontologies into practice, for example, Open Annotation to model interpretations or EmotionML to model emotions.

A.1.1.1.4. Generic methods of modeling

More and more used in the field of architecture, the generic models of modeling are slowly beginning to appear in the digital humanities [BRA 15, SZO 15, BER 12]. The purpose of this monitoring phase is to specify which model is the most effective to satisfy the needs of the project.

A.1.1.1.5. Web development framework

This monitoring will allow for the specification of the project's technical frameworks, in particular, specifying the languages, libraries and frameworks, which will be used.

A.1.1.1.6. e-Education resources

The field of e-Education is particularly rich in specifications that in turn make the resources produced interoperable and multilingual. This monitoring phase will help define the most effective practices taking place in this field.

A.1.1.2. *Digitization of the corpus*

The digitization of the corpus is one of the main objectives of this project. This will be implemented by an international team of researchers who will collect documents related to digital pedagogical resources, and archive and describe them according to different indexing grids designed for specific uses: archiving, exhibition, pedagogy, publication, etc.

To start this work as quickly as possible, we will provide researchers with the Omeka-S[2] software on a dedicated server. This tool has the advantage of being open source and can quickly start the archiving process by making use of the standard Dublin Core indexing. To facilitate the use of this tool by researchers, we will provide face-to-face training for members of the international team during a workshop and then by correspondence via videoconference.

Throughout the duration of Omeka's use, we will offer assistance to answer questions from researchers who will use this tool. Following the recommendations that will be defined following the monitoring process, we will continue to use Omeka by enriching it with other indexing grids, or we will eventually migrate the data to another more efficient tool should one be discovered during the monitoring process.

A.1.1.3. *Development of the Collective Intelligence Platform*

The Collective Intelligence Platform (CIP) is composed of an ecosystem linking documents, actors (IT and human) and project concepts. In view of the extent of the process of analyzing the documents related to e-Education,

---

2 https://omeka.org/s/

we wish to involve university students or high school students to collect and consolidate the factual information of place, date and actors. Designed in the style of a serious game, this work would allow participants to gain expertise by gradually crossing the "levels" in order to arrive at the modeling of an interpretation. In addition to the scientific aspect of this work, which would make it possible to compensate for the shortcomings of digital tools by providing reliable data, such detailed work on a corpus segment would give students the opportunity to exercise their ability to reflect, to become familiar with the methods used by scientists, to value their work and to learn to discern from a document what is important from what is incidental. In short, we propose to organize the observation of e-Education bodies in the same manner that thousands of volunteers identify the biodiversity within gardens[3], etc., precisely the same way as the hundreds of amateur researchers organized into knowledge societies, before the digital era.

The objective of this ecosystem is to optimize the use of data according to the needs of different stakeholders by facilitating interoperability and multilingualism. To achieve this goal, we will develop semantic maps (see section 4.2) designed specifically for the project in collaboration with researchers from an international team. From these, users will be able to write complex data that respect the formalisms of Linked Open Data (see section 5.1.2.5) by simply clicking on these maps.

Designed to evolve according to the needs that researchers will express, the ecosystem will develop the following agile methods of SCRUM and Extreme Programming. A GitHub project will be set up to manage the development progress and the expression of needs, and to build a community of developers around the project. We will train the teams so that they can make the best use of this tool.

A.1.1.4. *Development of digital teaching resources*

The current excitement surrounding the use of digital tools in education is reflected in numerous initiatives at all levels of training, from the first cycles to higher education; likewise in the context of professional training where, for example, serious games are multiplying. These developments now take the form of complex information ecosystems, where digital technologies blend with traditional pedagogical methods, where standards and techniques evolve towards more and more interoperability, and where institutions put in

---

3 Link to the French garden observatory: http://obj.mnhn.fr/

place observation tools for the evaluation of digital learning resources (DLRs).

Despite the importance of political, pedagogical and industrial challenges, there are many obstacles to the development of digital education, including:

– research on new forms of pedagogy induced by digital technology, evaluation of these pedagogies;

– teacher support for digital integration;

– interoperability of resources;

– copyrights;

– the protection of privacy;

– the structuring of supply and demand.

Our goal will be to show how to develop a knowledge ecosystem that, as these developments evolve, will:

– refine digital pedagogical needs through operational monitoring;

– train students in the creation of digital resources that respect interoperability standards;

– provide the economic sector with a pool of young designers and companies with students through professionalization and/or apprenticeship contracts;

– support teachers in the use of digital resources;

– provide researchers with a methodological framework for the field experimentation of innovative teaching resources.

In order to achieve these goals, the design and development team, in collaboration with the CIP and international teams, will use the e-Education corpus to design, build and test DLRs. The goal is not to compete with pedagogical platforms, like Moodle, but to provide resources for this type of platform. In the same manner as platform development, DLRs will be produced using agile development processes.

A.1.1.5. *Valorization and dissemination of the corpus and results*

In parallel with the work of researchers on the collective intelligence platform and the development of digital pedagogical resources, this project aims to enhance and disseminate the body of work and results. In order to do this, we organize our contribution into several sub-objectives.

A.1.1.5.1. Public consultation site

This site will be the "showcase" of the project. It will be accessible to all members of the project team so as to propose content that will be published after an editorial validation. Through this site, the public will be able to consult the corpus, the pedagogical resources and all the other productions generated by the project (reports, publications, generic tools, etc.). Developed from a multilingual CMS, the content will be consultable in the languages of the team members: English, Arabic, Catalan, Chinese, Creole, Spanish, French, Italian, Polish, etc.

A.1.1.5.2. Community management

An important part of the work of valorization and diffusion happens today through social networks. We will contribute to the publicity of the project by creating groups and publishing information on different social networks. The first part of this objective will be fulfilled through the common networks like Facebook, Google+ and Twitter onto which will be published the news of the project. A second part will be dedicated to the use of specialized networks, such as Zotero for bibliographic references, Diigo for web site monitoring and GitHub for IT development management.

As the project progresses, it will also be broadcast on specialized mailing lists for education and cultural communities, such as the *la liste culture multimédia*[4] (the multimedia culture list) or *la liste humanités numériques*[5] (the digital humanities list).

A.1.1.5.3. Publications and scientific conferences

The scientific work produced during the project will be presented in international conferences and published in journals or collective works. A global strategy will be defined with all project participants to define the topics that will be the subject of presentations and/or publications.

---

4 http://lists.imaginationforpeople.org/cgi-bin/mailman/listinfo/cmm
5 https://groupes.renater.fr/sympa/info/dh

A.1.2. *Activities*

We will describe the project activities here by presenting the general timeline, the management of human resources and the description of the tasks.

A.1.2.1. *General timeline of the project*

This package takes place over four academic years. The overall organization of activities during this period takes place according to the schedule below:

Activities related to the objectives	YR 1	YR 2	YR 3	YR 4
Monitoring of Science and Technology	X			
Digitalization of the Corpus	X	X	X	X
CIP Development		X	X	
CIP Maintenance				X
DLR Development		X	X	
DLR Maintenance				X
Valorization and Dissemination of the Corpus		X	X	X

Table A.1. *General timeline of the project*

A.1.2.2. *Human resources*

A.1.2.2.1. Internal package resources

The internal team of this project is composed of:

– three people managing the project, the strategic orientations, the relations with the international team, the technical and scientific expertise:

- Samuel Szoniecky, MCF Paris 8, Paragraphe Laboratory;

- a project administration officer (IGR);

- a research engineer (IGR);

– international project teams to digitize and capture metadata;

– one post-doctoral fellow or research engineer responsible for monitoring and writing reports;

– one Web designer dealing with the design of the CIP, DLR and documentation;

– one pedagogical engineer working on the design of DLRs;

– ten 'Masters 2' research assistants attending digital humanities courses at Paris 8 University or partner universities will work in pairs to develop and maintain the CIP and DLRs. They will be technically supervised by the research engineer and the web designer. Pedagogical supervision will be provided by Samuel Szoniecky.

All these people will work full-time on the project, except for trainees who will work on the project for 50% of their first semester so as to be able to take the courses alternately. The activity of these people takes place globally according to the semester schedule below:

People linked with objectives	S. 1	S. 2	S. 3	S. 4	S. 5	S. 6	S. 7	S. 8
Samuel Szoniecky	X	X	X	X	X	X	X	X
Project Administrator	X	X	X	X	X	X	X	X
Research Engineer	X	X	X	X	X	X	X	X
International Team	X	X	X	X	X	X	X	X
Post-doctorate/IGE	X	X	X	X				
Pedagogical Engineer		X	X	X	X	X		
Web Designer			X	X	X	X		
Research Assistants 1 and 2			X	X				
Research Assistants 3 and 4			X	X				
Research Assistants 5 and 6					X	X		
Research Assistants 7 and 8					X	X		
Research Assistants 9 and 10							X	X

Table A.2. *Project human resources*

A.1.2.2.2. External resources

External resources are mainly composed of:

– members of the volunteer teaching teams to test the DLR;

– volunteers interested in the project and wishing to participate in its development (crowdsourcing).

A.1.2.3. *Description of tasks*

Here is the detailed list of tasks that will be performed in this package:

– WBS 1.1 Monitoring of science and technology (see section A.1.1.1 for more details)

– WBS 1.2 Digitization of the corpus (see section A.1.1.2 for more details)

– WBS 1.2.1 Installation and configuration of the server

The research engineer will be responsible for installing and setting up the high-performance web server that will be used throughout the project. A reference document will be written to describe the specific characteristics of this server. This server will initially be hosted at Paris 8 and will be able to migrate according to the results of the technology monitoring phase.

– WBS 1.2.2 Omeka

– WBS 1.2.2.1 Installation and configuration of Omeka

The research engineer will be tasked with installing the server and configuring the Omeka CMS, in particular to:

– define the collections;

– define the metadata;

– create user accounts;

– install the necessary extensions.

A reference document will be written to describe the precise settings of this installation. It will be made available on GitHub.

– WBS 1.2.2.2 Formation of the team at Omeka

Training will be given to project team members, so that they can quickly begin the digitization of the corpus. This training will take the form of a one-day workshop for available team members and will be followed by videoconference training for those who could not reach the workshop.

– WBS 1.2.2.3 Omeka assistance

Throughout the duration of the project, the research engineer will provide telephone or videoconferencing technical assistance for users via VR.

– WBS 1.2.3 Digitizing documents

Compared with Omeka, the task is to save the digitized work either by downloading it to the server or by indicating the link where the document is located.

– WBS 1.2.4 Entering metadata

In parallel with the digitization task, researchers will have to enter the metadata of each document. These metadata will initially be those corresponding to the Dublin Core, then, as the project progresses, other metadata grids will be built, for example, to describe pedagogical properties.

– WBS 1.3 Development of the Collective Intelligence Platform (see section A.1.13 for an overall description of this task)

– WBS 1.3.1 Implementation of the Open Source development tool

GitHub[6] is a very effective solution for collective development projects: managing source history; expressing needs; describing problems; providing technical documentation; creating a developer community; and so on.

– WBS 1.3.2 Training the team at GitHub

Training will be given to members of the internal team for this project, so that they can manage developments as well as to members of the international team, so that they can express their needs or mention the bugs.

– WBS 1.3.3 Expression of scientific needs

The expression of the scientific needs will be done via GitHub to collect in the same tool at the same time, the requests, the reflections around these requests and their developments.

– WBS 1.3.4 PIC sprints

As stated in section A.1.1.3, IT developments will be done according to the combination of SCRUM and Extreme Programming. The principle is to multiply the development cycles (sprint) on the collective intelligence platform (CIP) according to the following process:

1) Definition of scenarios = 1 day. From the expressions of needs made on GitHub, the scenarios will be described to specify the functionalities that can be developed during the cycle.

2) Functional test specifications = 2 days. The scenarios will be detailed in as many functional tests as needed to validate for the scenario being sought after.

3) Completion of tasks = 20 days. Features are expanded until all functional tests are passed.

---

6 For more detail, visit: https://guides.github.com

4) Documentation = 2 days. The project documentation is updated to reflect the latest developments.

5) Delivery = 1 day. The new features are put into production on the platform.

We have planned 18 development sprints in years 2 and 3.

– WBS 1.3.5 Corrective maintenance

Corrective maintenance will be provided until the end of the project.

– WBS 1.4 Development of digital pedagogy resources (see section A.1.1.4 for an overall description of this task)

– WBS 1.4.1 DPR sprints

Digital pedagogy resources (DPRs) will be developed following the same principles as those applied for the CIP. However, in the case of DPRs, we enrich the process with a step corresponding to the experimentation of the resource in a pedagogical framework and we increase the time necessary for the definition of scenarios and documentation. This explains why there are only 10 DPR sprints.

1) Definition of scenarios = 10 days.

2) Functional test specifications = 2 days.

3) Completion of tasks = 20 days.

4) In situ experiments = 10 days. The DPR developed will be tested in a classroom in collaboration with the teaching teams.

5) Documentation = 2 days.

6) Delivery = 1 day (available on the server or on an app store for tablets or smartphones).

We planned to do 10 development sprints in years 2 and 3.

– WBS 1.4.2 Corrective maintenance

Corrective maintenance will be provided until the end of the project.

– WBS 1.5 Valorization and dissemination of the corpus and results (see section A.1.1.5 for a description of this task)

A.1.2.4. *Products created through the project*

In this project, all the products we produce will be licensed under Creative Commons Attribution - SharingAlike: CC BY-SA[7]. Here is the list of products:

1) Monitoring report on archival platforms for scientific data.

2) Monitoring report on domain ontologies.

3) Monitoring report on interoperable languages for the human sciences.

4) Monitoring report on generic modeling methods.

5) Monitoring report on Web development frameworks.

6) Monitoring report on e-Education resources.

7) Specifications of the Collective Intelligence Platform.

8) Collective Intelligence Platform:

a) source codes;

b) documentation.

9) Digital pedagogical resources:

a) source codes;

b) executable versions;

c) documentation.

10) Scientific articles.

11) Collective works.

A.1.2.5. *The GANTT of its realization*

Here is a Gantt chart that summarizes the planning for this project[8]:

---

7 https://creativecommons.org/licenses/by-sa/3.0/

8 For more details on the tasks, the allocation of resources and the costs, you can consult the online version here: http://gapai.univparis8.fr/ACTA/gantt/html/

You can also view the Gantt by opening the Gantter tool here: http://gapai.univparis8.fr/ACTA/gantt/GanttACTA.gantter

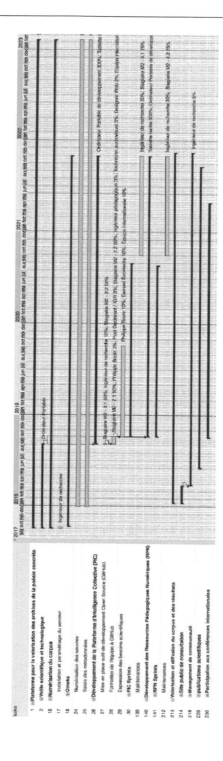

Figure A.1. *The Gantt of the project. For a color version of the figure, see www.iste.co.uk/szoniecky/ecosystems.zip*

Posts	Cost		Year 1	Year 2	Year 3	Year 4	TOTAL
Personnel costs							
	Occupation	Monthly					
Samuel Szoniecky	20%	4,458.97	10,701.53	10,701.53	10,701.53	10,701.53	**42,806.12**
Administration Manager	100%	2,879.28	34,551.36	34,551.36	34,551.36	34,551.36	**138,205.44**
Research Engineer	100%	2,879.28	34,551.36	34,551.36	34,551.36	34,551.36	**138,205.44**
Post-Doctorate/IGE	100%	2,583.80	31,005.60	31,005.60	31,005.60	31,005.60	**124,022.40**
Pedagogical Engineer	100%	2,583.80	7,751.40	31,005.60	31,005.60	31,005.60	**100,768.20**
Web Designer	100%	2,583.80		31,005.60	31,005.60	31,005.60	**93,016.80**
Research Assistants	75%	555.00		19,980.00	19,980.00	9,990.00	**49,950.00**
Purchase of supplies/consumables							
Stationery			100.00	100.00	100.00	100.00	**400.00**
Documentation			200.00	200.00	200.00	200.00	**800.00**
Software Licenses			1,000.00	1,000.00	1,000.00	1,000.00	**4,000.00**
Mission expenses							
Training Workshop			3,000.00				**3,000.00**
International Conference				2,000.00	2,000.00	2,000.00	**6,000.00**
Equipment	**Unit**						
Web Server		8,000.00	8, 000.00				**8,000.00**
Laptop Computer		1,600.00	3, 200,00				**3,200,00**
Development Computer		2,500.00	5, 000.00	12,500.00			**17,500.00**
Touch Pad		400.00		2,400.00			**2,400.00**
TOTAL			139,061.25	211,001.05	196,101.05	186,111.05	732,274.40

Table A.3. *Project budget*

A.1.3. *Budget*

This indicative budget gives priority to the finances needed to develop this project. It will probably have to be refined according to the priorities that will be given and the evolution of salary scales. The sums are in euros.

A.1.4. *Results evaluation criteria*

A.1.4.1. *Risks*

A number of risks have been identified for the project and alternatives are proposed to address them. We identified two types of risks: technical risks and human risks.

A.1.4.1.1. Technical risks

– Poor efficiency of technology monitoring. This risk may be related to a lack of sufficient time devoted to monitoring, or a partial mismatch between the monitoring objectives and the needs of the project. We have overcome the first risk by devoting a full year to the previous and the second by deploying from the beginning of the project an internal server and an Omeka platform. This will allow the team to quickly start the digitization of the corpus as they go, which will redirect the monitoring if necessary.

– Failure of delivery. This risk appears in V methodologies that start with a complete specification of the requirement and end with a delivery. The use of an agile method results in partial deliveries. This methodology is reflected in the project by the implementation of sprints.

– Overflow of tasks. This risk exists for sprints. A sprint may not finish on the desired date. In this case, we will reassign to the following sprint the inconclusive functional tests. If this solution is insufficient, we will reduce the number of sprints and increase their duration.

– Difficulty of pedagogical experimentation: partner universities commit themselves to encourage teams interested in experimental poetry to participate in this experiment. The teachers involved in the project will also involve their students in these experiments, especially during writing workshops.

– Sustainability of the project: technology monitoring will determine the free platform best suited to the project. The risk is that this type of solution works for the data but not for the pedagogical tools or the project site that will require maintenance. We foresee in the budget a maintenance period of 5 years after the end of the project, which will be subcontracted by the Paragraphe laboratory of Paris 8.

A.1.4.1.2. Human risks

– Dissociation risk of the package with the scientific packages. This risk would correspond to an isolation of the computer question in the project. It can appear when the project considers the digital as a simple tool and not an intrinsic component of the project. This risk will be avoided in many ways. The digital package team is involved in the project team and, as such, it participates in all project meetings and project dynamics starting from the pre-project phase. In addition, a member of the team (Samuel Szoniecky) will also be active in the choice of the corpus and in the analysis phases. Finally, the digital project has a real research question related to indexing and semantic mapping, making it a scientific project and not only a technical one.

– Risk of misunderstanding or misuse of tools by stakeholders. This concerns the members of the international team and research assistants. In order to mitigate this risk, the project includes training days and personalized assistance. The research assistants will also be aware of the project and will acquire during the course the prerequisites necessary for their intervention. That is why we prefer to hire students from our courses.

– Long absence of a team member: if temporary replacement of a member is necessary, we will first approach the competent services located in the partner universities to take charge of the task in a distributed way. We are constantly documenting the project in order to facilitate a replacement in such an event. Depending on the tasks to be accomplished, we also have the possibility of proposing short ancillary projects that can be financed by the laboratory or by *BQR* (internal funding at the university), or even by the *labex ArtsH2H* if the need for funding becomes important. These solutions allow for the temporary hiring of a substitute to make up for the absence.

– Departure of a permanent member of the laboratory (MCF). This risk is almost zero over the duration of the project. If it occurs, the remaining permanent members adjust their overall university research time to take over the activities of the outgoing member, in addition to their own, or else the laboratory shall assign to the project one of its members to replace the outgoing member. In any case, the Paragraphe laboratory plans to carry out the project regardless of the personnel who devote themselves and their time to it.

Bibliography

[ALB 17] ALBERT J.-P., KEDZIERSKA-MANZON A., "Des objets-signes aux objets-sujets", *Archives de sciences sociales des religions*, no. 174, pp. 13–25, 2017.

[AMI 10] AMIEL P.H.L., *Ethnométhodologie appliquée: éléments de sociologie praxéologique*, Presses du LEMA, Saint-Denis, 2010.

[ANG 15] ANGELINI L., ABOU KHALED O., MUGELLINI E., "EmotiPlant: facilitating human-plant interaction for older adults", *27ᵉ Conférence francophone sur l'interaction Homme-Machine*, Toulouse, France, p. 14, available at: https://hal.archives-ouvertes.fr/hal-01219106v1, 2015.

[ANT 09] ANTOINE M., *Zen & Connaissance: Vers une écologie spirituelle*, Éditions Oxus, Toulouse, 2009.

[ARR 15] ARRUABARRENA B., "L'écosystème numérique de la datavisualisation", *I2D – Information, données & documents*, vol. 52, no. 2, pp. 56–58, 2015.

[ASS 16] ASSENS C., ENSMINGER J., "Une typologie des écosystèmes d'affaires: de la confiance territoriale aux plateformes sur Internet", *Vie & sciences de l'entreprise*, no. 200, pp. 77–98, 2016.

[AUT 99] AUTHIER M., LÉVY P., *Les Arbres de connaissances*, La Découverte, Paris, 1999.

[AVE 13] AVERLANT P., "Arbres de connaissances et chemins de l'expérience", *VST – Vie sociale et traitements*, no. 119, pp. 142–144, 2013.

[BAB 10] BABOU I., Rationalité & nature. Une approche communicationnelle, HDR, Paris-Diderot University, Paris, 2010.

[BAC 07] BACHIMONT B., *Ingénierie des connaissances et des contenus: le numérique entre ontologies et documents*, Hermès-Lavoisier, Paris, 2007.

[BAC 10] BACHELARD G., "Rêverie et radio", *Le Droit de rêver*, PUF, Paris, 2010.

[BAL 96] BALPE J.-P., *Techniques avancées pour l'hypertexte*, Hermès, Paris, 1996.

[BAL 02] BALPE J.-P., "La programmation du sens", *université de tous les savoirs, volume 5: Le Cerveau, le langage, le sens*, Odile Jacob, Paris, 2002.

[BAT 96] BATESON G., *Une unité sacrée: quelques pas de plus vers une écologie de l'esprit*, Le Seuil, Paris, 1996.

[BAT 05] BATT N., "L'expérience diagrammatique: un nouveau régime de pensée", *Penser Par Le Diagramme: De Gilles Deleuze à Gilles Châtelet*, Presses universitaires de Vincennes, Saint-Denis, 2005.

[BAT 08] BATESON G., "Crise dans l'écologie de l'esprit", *Vers une écologie de l'esprit: Tome 2*, Le Seuil, Paris, 2008.

[BAU 06] BAUMAN Z., *La Vie liquide*, Le Rouergue, Rodez, 2006.

[BAU 14] BAUDRY B., MONPERRUS M., MONY C. et al., "DIVERSIFY: ecology-inspired software evolution for diversity emergence", *Proceedings of the International Conference on Software Maintenance and Reengineering (CSMR)*, Belgium, pp. 444–447, 2014.

[BER 93] BERQUE A., *Du geste à la cité*, Gallimard, Paris, 1993.

[BER 97] BERQUE A., "Entretiens avec Augustin Berque", available at: http://urbanisme.u-pec.fr/documentation/paroles/augustin-berque-64743.kjsp, 1997.

[BER 99] BERTIN J., *Sémiologie graphique: les diagrammes, les réseaux, les cartes*, Éditions de l'EHESS, Paris, 1999.

[BER 00] BERQUE A., *Logique du lieu et dépassement de la modernité, volume 1: Nishida: La Mouvance philosophique*, Ousia, Brussels, 2000.

[BER 09a] BERQUE A., *Écoumène: Introduction à l'étude des milieux humains*, Belin, Paris, 2009.

[BER 09b] BERNS T., *Gouverner sans gouverner: Une archéologie politique de la statistique*, PUF, Paris, 2009.

[BER 10] BERQUE A., *Milieu et identité humaine: Notes pour un dépassement de la modernité*, Éditions donner lieu, Paris, 2010.

[BER 11] BERQUE A., "Cosmos malade?", *Philosophie magazine, Le cosmos des philosophes*, special edition, no. 9, 2011.

[BER 12] BERQUE A., "La chôra chez Platon", *Espace et lieu dans la pensée occidentale de Platon à Nietzsche*, La Découverte, Paris, 2012.

[BER 13] BERTHELON F., *Modélisation et détection des émotions à partir de données expressives et contextuelles*, thesis, University of Nice - Sophia Antipolis, 2013.

[BES 06] BESSIS R., "La syntaxe des mondes. Éléments de classification des formes d'écologie symbolique", *Multitudes*, no. 24, pp. 53–61, available at: https://www.cairn.info/revue-multitudes-2006-1-page-53.htm, 2006.

[BLO 14] BLOOMFIELD C., LESAGE C., *Oulipo*, Gallimard, Paris, 2014.

[BOO 08] BOOTZ P., SZONIECKY S., "Toward an ontology of the field of digital poetry", *Electronic Literature in Europe*, University of Bergen, Norway, 2008.

[BOS 11] BOSTOCK M., OGIEVETSKY V., HEER J., "D3: data-driven documents", *IEEE Transactions on Visualization & Computer Graphics*, vol. 17, no. 12, pp. 2301–2309, 2011.

[BOS 14] BOSSEUR J.-Y., "L'école de New York", *Théories de la composition musicale au XXe siècle*, Symétrie, Lyon, 2014.

[BOU 89] BOULEZ P., *Le Pays fertile: Paul Klee*, Gallimard, Paris, 1989.

[BOU 01] BOURDIEU P., *Langage et pouvoir symbolique*, Le Seuil, Paris, 2001.

[BOU 11] BOUDON P., "La question du genre comme nœud de relations sémantiques", *Actes Semiotiques*, 2011, available at: http://epublications.unilim.fr/revues/as/1883.

[BOU 15] BOUTAUD J.-J., *Sensible et communication*, ISTE Éditions, London, 2015.

[BOU 16] BOUHAI N., "Pratiques et enjeux de la documentation numérique personnelle", *Colloque International sur les Bibliothèques et Archives à l'ère des Humanités Numériques (CIBAHN)*, Tunis, Tunisia, 2016.

[BRO 11] BROUDOUX E., FRANÇOIS C., BESAGNI D. *et al.*, "Références scientifiques en ligne : folksonomies et activité des groupes", *8e Colloque international de l'ISKO*, Lille, 2011.

[BRU 17] BRUN G., "Pouvoir d'agir, en analyse de l'activité", *Activités*, vol. 14, no. 1, available at: https://activites.revues.org/2957, 2017.

[CAR 99] CARD S.K., MACKINLAY J.D., SHNEIDERMAN B., *Readings in Information Visualization*, pp. 579–581, Morgan Kaufmann, San Francisco, CA, 1999.

[CHA 15] CHATEAURAYNAUD F., "Trajectoires argumentatives et constellations discursives", *Réseaux*, no. 188, pp. 121–158, 2015.

[CHO 94] CHOGYAM T., *Mandala. Un chaos ordonné*, Points, Paris, 1994.

[CHU 13] CHU S., QUEK F., "Information holodeck: thinking in technology ecologies", *14th International Conference on Human-Computer Interaction (INTERACT)*, vol. LNCS-8117, pp. 167–184, 2013.

[CIT 06] CITTON Y., "Noo-politique spinoziste?", *Multitudes*, vol. 27, no. 4, p. 203, 2006.

[CIT 08] CITTON Y., "Entre l'économie psychique de Spinoza et l'inter-psychologie économique de Tarde", *Spinoza et les sciences sociales: de la puissance de la multitude à l'économie des affects*, Éditions Amsterdam, Paris, 2008.

[CIT 10] CITTON Y., *L'Avenir des humanités: Économie de la connaissance ou cultures de l'interprétation?*, La Découverte, Paris, 2010.

[CIT 14] CITTON Y., *Pour une écologie de l'attention*, Le Seuil, Paris, 2014.

[CIT 16] CITTON Y., "Revenu inconditionnel d'existence et économie générale de l'attention", *Multitudes*, no. 63, pp. 59–71, 2016.

[CLO 08] CLOT Y., *Travail et pouvoir d'agir,* PUF, Paris, 2008.

[CNN 15] CONSEIL NATIONAL DU NUMÉRIQUE (CNN), Ambition numérique: pour une politique française et européenne de la transition numérique, 2015.

[COL 98] COLLECTIF, *Revue d'esthétique*, nos 13–15, John Cage, 1998.

[COL 05] COLLECTIF, *Vers les sociétés du savoir*, Unesco, 2005.

[COR 11] CORDIER A., "La recherche d'information sur Internet des collégiens: entre imaginaires, pratiques et prescriptions", *Documentaliste – Sciences de l'Information*, no. 48, March 2011.

[COU 43] COURNOT A.A., *Exposition de la théorie des chances et des probabilités*, 1843.

[COU 14] COUTANT A., DOMENGET J.-C., "Un cadre épistémologique pour enquêter sur les dispositifs sociotechniques d'information et de communication", in BOURDELOIE H., DOUYERE D. (eds), *Méthodes de recherche sur l'information et la communication*, Éditions Mare et Martin, Paris, 2014.

[DAR 01] DARRAS B., "Les formes du savoir et l'éducation aux images", *Recherches en communication*, vol. 16, no. 16, pp. 153–166, 2001.

[DE 89] DE DUVE T., *Au nom de l'art*, Éditions de Minuit, Paris, 1989.

[DE 97] DE CHARDIN P.T., TARDIVEL F., *Hymne de l'univers*, Le Seuil, Paris, 1997.

[DEB 16] DEBOURDEAU A., "Aux origines de la pensée écologique: Ernst Haeckel, du naturalisme à la philosophie de l'Oikos", *Revue française d'histoire des idées politiques*, no. 44, pp. 33–62, 2016.

[DEC 03] DECHARNEUX B., NEFONTAINE L., *Le Symbole,* PUF, Paris, 2003.

[DEL 68] DELEUZE G., *Spinoza et le problème de l'expression*, Éditions de Minuit, Paris, 1968.

[DEL 80] DELEUZE G., GUATTARI F., *Mille plateaux*, Éditions de Minuit, Paris, 1980.

[DEL 88] DELEUZE G., *Le pli*, Editions de Minuit, 1988.

[DEL 01] DELEUZE G., *Spinoza : immortalité et éternité*, Gallimard, Paris, 2001.

[DEL 03] DELEUZE G., *Spinoza : Philosophie pratique*, Éditions de Minuit, 2003.

[DEM 00] DEMANGEOT J., *Les Milieux "naturels " du globe*, Armand Colin, Paris, 2000.

[DES 05] DESCOLA P., *Par-delà nature et culture*, Gallimard, Paris, 2005.

[DES 06] DESCOLA P., "La fabrique des images", *Anthropologie et Sociétés*, vol. 30, no. 3, pp. 167–182, 2006.

[DES 10] DESCOLA P. (ed.), *La Fabrique des images: Visions du monde et formes de la représentation*, Somogy éditions d'art, Paris, 2010.

[DES 11] DESCOLA P., *L'Écologie des autres: l'anthropologie et la question de la nature*, Éditions Quæ, Versailles, 2011.

[DES 13] DESFRICHES DORIA O., La classification à facettes pour la gestion des connaissances métier: méthodologie d'élaboration de FolkClassifications à facettes, PhD thesis, CNAM, Paris, 2013.

[DJE 16] DJELIL F., Conception et évaluation d'un micromonde de programmation orientée-objet fondé sur un jeu de construction et d'animation 3D, PhD thesis, université Blaise Pascal, Clermont-Ferrand II, 2016.

[DUB 90] DUBOIS D., *Le Labyrinthe de l'intelligence*, Academia, Louvain, 1990.

[DUC 08] DUCHEMIN S., Vers une écologie spirituelle de la ville: Pour une critique du développement durable urbain, approches philosophique et psychanalytique, université de Nancy 2, 2008.

[DUP 11] DUPIRE J., "Jeu sérieux, révolution pédagogique ou effet de mode", *Revue d'intelligence artificielle, RSTI série RIA*, Hermès-Lavoisier, Paris, 2011.

[DUR 99] Dury P., "Étude comparative et diachronique des concepts ecosystem et écosystème", *Meta*, vol. 44, no. 3, pp. 485–499, 1999.

[ECO 79] Eco U., *L'Œuvre ouverte*, Le Seuil, Paris, 1979.

[ECO 94a] Eco U., *Les Limites de l'interprétation*, Le Livre de Poche, Paris, 1994.

[ECO 94b] Eco U., *La Recherche de la langue parfaite dans la culture européenne*, Le Seuil, Paris, 1994.

[EDE 15] Edeline F., Klinkenberg J.-M., *Principia semiotica: aux sources du sens*, Les Impressions nouvelles, Brussels, 2015.

[ERT 09] Ertzscheid O., "L'homme, un document comme les autres", *Hermès, La Revue*, vol. 53, no. 1, pp. 33–40, 2009.

[ERT 11] Ertzscheid O., "Méthodes, techniques et outils. Qu'y aura-t-il demain sous nos moteurs?", *Documentaliste – Sciences de l'Information*, vol. 48, no. 3, pp. 10–11, 2011.

[FAD 16] Fadda E., "Graphes, diagrammes, langue et pensée chez C.S. Peirce", *Dossiers d'HEL*, vol. 9, pp. 98–112, 2016.

[FAV 16] Favier L., Mustafa El Hadi W., Vinck D., "Interopérabilité culturelle", *Communication. Information médias théories pratiques*, vol. 34, no. 1, August 2016.

[FER 09] Ferber J., "Vers un modèle multi-agent de construction d'ontologie", *Ontologie et dynamique des systèmes complexes, perspectives interdisciplinaires*, Rochebrune, France, 2009.

[FER 14] Ferre S., Reconciling expressivity and usability in information access, HDR, University of Rennes 1, 2014.

[FOL 04] Folch H., Habert B., "Langages de métadonnées pour Web(s) sémantique(s)", in Ihadjadene M. (ed.), *Méthodes avancées pour les systèmes de recherche d'informations*, Hermès-Lavoisier, Paris, 2004.

[FRO 13] Froissart P., "Information and communication studies: a scientific cartography", in Olivesi S. (ed.), *Sciences de l'information et de la communication*, pp. 269–294, Presses universitaires de Grenoble, 2013.

[GAL 14] Gallant K., Lorang E., Ramirez A., "Tools for the digital humanities: a librarian's guide", *proposed by Anneka Ramirez 9 December*, 2014.

[GAN 93] Ganascia J.-G., *L'Intelligence artificielle*, Flammarion, Paris, 1993.

[GAN 08] Gandon F., Graphes RDF et leur manipulation pour la gestion de connaissances, HDR, INRIA Sophia Antipolis, Nice, 2008.

[GAU 01] GAUFEY L.G., *L'Incomplétude du symbolique: de René Descartes à Jacques Lacan*, EPEL, Paris, 2001.

[GLE 99] GLEICK J., *La Théorie du chaos: vers une nouvelle science*, Flammarion, Paris, 1999.

[GRI 16] GRINEVALD J., "Le développement de/dans la biosphère", *L'Homme inachevé: un devenir à construire: les "possibles" de l'homme*, pp. 29–44, Graduate Institute Publications, Geneva, 2016.

[GUA 89a] GUATTARI F., *Cartographies schizoanalytiques*, Galilée, Paris, 1989.

[GUA 89b] GUATTARI F., *Les Trois Écologies*, Galilée, Paris, 1989.

[GUA 92] GUATTARI F., *Chaosmose*, Galilée, Paris, 1992.

[GUE 12] GUERIN J., ALBERO B., DURAND M., *Activité collective et apprentissage: de l'ergonomie à l'écologie des situations de formation*, L'Harmattan, Paris, 2012.

[HAC 12] HACHOUR H., SZONIECKY S., BOUHAI N., "The role of semantic topology in sensmaking processes: addressing challenges of indexing with metalanguages", *22nd European-Japanese Conference on Information Modeling and Knowledge Bases*, Prague, Czech Republic, pp. 244–257, 2012.

[HAC 14] HACHOUR H., SZONIECKY S., "Impact des TIC sur la visibilité des SIC à l'international: analyses sémantiques d'un corpus de communiqués diplomatiques", *XIXᵉ Congrès de la SFSIC, Penser les techniques et les technologies*, University Sud Toulon-Var, 2014.

[HEN 14] HENRI F., "Les environnements personnels d'apprentissage, étude d'une thématique de recherche en émergence", *Revue STICEF*, no. 21, December 2014.

[HES 02] HESSE H., *Le Jeu des perles de verre*, Le Livre de Poche, Paris, 2002.

[HOF 13] HOFSTADTER D., SANDER E., *L'Analogie : cœur de la pensée*, Odile Jacob, Paris, 2013.

[HUT 00] HUTZLER G., Du jardin des hasards aux jardins de données: une approche artistique et multi-agent des interfaces homme/systèmes complexes, PhD thesis, Computer Science, University Paris 6, 2000.

[ILL 75] ILLICH I., *La Convivialité*, Le Seuil, Paris, 1975.

[IMB 14] IMBERT J.-P., Adaptation du design des visualisations de type supervisions pour optimiser la transmission des notifications classées par niveau d'intérêt, PhD thesis, ISAE, Toulouse, 2014.

[ING 12] INGOLD T., MADELIN P., CHARBONNIER P., "Culture, nature et environnement", *Tracés*, vol. 22, no. 1, pp. 169–187, 2012.

[ING 17] INGOLD T., AFEISSA H.-S., GOSSELIN S., "Les matériaux de la vie", *Multitudes*, no. 65, pp. 51–58, 2017.

[ITO 16] ITO J., HOWE J., *Whiplash: How to Survive Our Faster Future*, Grand Central Publishing, New York, 2016.

[JAC 07] JACOB C., *Lieux de savoir: Tome 1, Espaces et communautés*, Albin Michel, Paris, 2007.

[JAT 16] JATON F., VINCK D., "Processus frictionnels de mises en bases de données", *Revue d'anthropologie des connaissances*, vol. 11, no. 4, pp. 489–504, 2016.

[JAV 16] JAVEAU A., L'information en tant que lien essentiel entre les sciences de la nature et les sciences humaines: axe principal: incidences de l'information sur le fonctionnement et le comportement de l'homme considéré en tant que structure dissipative, PhD thesis, University of Burgundy, 2016.

[JEA 00] JEANNERET Y., "La trivialité comme évidence et comme problème. À propos de la querelle des impostures", *Enjeux de l'information et de la communication*, available at: http://www.ugrenoble3.fr/les_enjeux/2000/Jeanneret/index.html, 2000.

[JEA 07] JEANNERET Y., *Y a-t-il (vraiment) des technologies de l'information?*, Presses universitaires du Septentrion, Villeneuve d'Ascq, 2007.

[JEA 14] JEANNERET Y., *Critique de la trivialité: les médiations de la communication, enjeu de pouvoir*, Éditions Non Standard, Paris, 2014.

[JED 07] JEDRZEJEWSKI F., Diagrammes et Catégories, PhD thesis, Philosophy, Paris-Diderot University, 2007.

[JOS 11] JOSSET R., "Inconscient collectif et noosphère. Du "monde imaginal" au "village global"", *Sociétés*, vol. 111, no. 1, p. 35, 2011.

[JUA 10] JUANALS B., NOYER J.-M., "De l'émergence de nouvelles technologies intellectuelles", in JUANALS B., NOYER J.-M. (eds), *Technologies de l'information et intelligences collectives*, Hermès-Lavoisier, Paris, 2010.

[JUA 16] JUANALS B., MINEL J.-L., "La construction d'un espace patrimonial partagé dans le Web de données ouvert", *Communication. Information médias théories pratiques*, vol. 34, no. 1, August 2016.

[JUN 88] JUNG G.C., *Synchronicité et Paracelsica*, Albin Michel, Paris, 1988.

[KEM 14] KEMBELLEC G., CHARTRON G., SALEH I., *Recommender Systems*, ISTE Ltd, London and John Wiley & Sons, New York, 2014.

[KLA 09] KLANTEN R., *Data Flow: Design graphique et visualisation d'information*, Thames & Hudson, London, 2009.

[LAC 09] LACOUR S., La trajectivité de l'Ahvp, l'animation historique vivante du patrimoine, une pratique ascendante et "transmunicante" élément de structuration et de singularisation du territoire, PhD thesis, université Paris-Est, École doctorale ICMS, Marne-la-Vallée, 2009.

[LAF 15] LAFOURCADE M., LE BRUN N., JOUBERT A., *Games with a Purpose (GWAPs)*, ISTE Ltd, London and John Wiley & Sons, New York, 2015.

[LAT 12] LATOUR B., *Enquêtes sur les modes d'existence: une anthropologie des Modernes*, La Découverte, Paris, 2012.

[LAT 13] LATOUR B., JENSEN P., VENTURINI T. *et al.*, "Le tout est toujours plus petit que ses parties", *Réseaux*, vol. 177, no. 1, pp. 197–232, April 2013.

[LAT 15] LATOUR B., *Face à Gaïa*, La Découverte, Paris, 2015.

[LAV 09] LAVAUD-FOREST S., "Perspectives numériques. Variabilités, interactions, univers distribués", *Communications*, vol. 85, no. 2, pp. 55–64, October 2009.

[LEA 98] LEARY F.T., *Chaos et cyberculture*, Éditions du Lézard, Paris, 1998.

[LEL 09] LELEU-MERVIEL S., USEILLE P., "Some revisions on the concept of information", in PAPY F. (ed.), *Information Science*, ISTE Ltd, London and John Wiley & Sons, New York, 2009.

[LEN 14] LENKA S., SZONIECKY S., "L'usage des diagrammes dans les partitions musicales: du graphique au conceptuel pour une potentialité du geste", *XIXe Congrès de la SFSIC, Penser les techniques et les technologies*, University Sud Toulon-Var, 2014.

[LEO 17] LEONARD L.J., "Écologie (socio) linguistique: évolution, élaboration et variation, (Socio) linguistic Ecology: Progression, Development and Variation", *Langage et société*, nos 160–161, pp. 267–282, May 2017.

[LÉV 03] LÉVY P., "Le jeu de l'intelligence collective", *Sociétés*, vol. 1, no. 79, pp. 105–122, 2003.

[LÉV 11] LÉVY P., *The Semantic Sphere 1*, ISTE Ltd, London and John Wiley & Sons, New York, 2011.

[LIM 10] LIMPENS F., Multi-points of view semantic enrichment of folksonomies, PhD thesis, Informatique, University Nice Sophia Antipolis, École doctorale STIC, 2010.

[LIP 06] LIPOVETSKY G., *Les Temps hypermodernes*, Le Livre de Poche, Paris, 2006.

[LIQ 11] LIQUETE V., Des pratiques d'information à la construction de connaissances en contexte: de l'analyse à la modélisation SEPICRI, HDR, University of Rouen, 2011.

[LYO 79] LYOTARD J.-F., *La Condition postmoderne*, Éditions de Minuit, Paris, 1979.

[MAD 15] MADER S., Le "game design" de jeux thérapeutiques: modèles et méthodes pour la conception du gameplay, PhD thesis, Computer science, CNAM, Paris, 2015.

[MAL 98] MALLARMÉ S., *Œuvres complètes*, Gallimard, Paris, 1998.

[MAN 15] MANSOURI B., Normes internationales élargies et dépassement du calcul de la valeur, PhD thesis, University of Bordeaux, 2015.

[MAT 94] MATURANA H.R., VARELA F.J., *L'Arbre de la connaissance*, Editions Addison-Wesley France, Paris, 1994.

[MEL 06] MELANÇON G., "Espaces collaboratifs métaphores graphiques et exploration visuelle", *Intelligence collective rencontre*, pp. 37–42, 2006.

[MOR 81] MORIN E., *La Méthode, tome 1*, Le Seuil, Paris, 1981.

[MOR 85] MORIN E., *La Méthode, La Vie de la vie, tome 2*, Le Seuil, Paris, 1985.

[MOR 92] MORIN E., *La Méthode, La Connaissance de la connaissance, tome 3*, Le Seuil, Paris, 1992.

[MOR 95] MORIN E., *La Méthode, Les Idées, tome 4*, Le Seuil, Paris, 1995.

[MOR 99] MORIN E., *Relier les connaissances*, Le Seuil, Paris, 1999.

[MOR 01] MORIN E., *La Méthode, l'humanité de l'humanité, tome 5: L'Identité humaine*, Le Seuil, Paris, 2001.

[MOR 06] MORIN E., *La Méthode, Éthique, tome 6*, Points, Paris, 2006.

[MOU 06] MOULIER-BOUTANG Y., NEYRAT F., VIDECOQ E., "Construire de nouvelles relations avec…", *Multitudes*, vol. 24, no. 1, pp. 19–27, 2006.

[MOU 10] MOULIER-BOUTANG Y., *L'Abeille et l'Économiste*, Carnets Nord, Paris, 2010.

[MUG 06] MUGUR-SCHÄCHTER M., *Sur le tissage des connaissances*, Hermès-Lavoisier, Paris, 2006.

[NEF 09] NEF F., *Traité d'ontologie à l'usage des non-philosophes*, Gallimard, Paris, 2009.

[NOY 10] NOYER J.-M., "Connaissance, pensée, réseaux à l'heure numérique", *Les Cahiers du numérique*, vol. 6, no. 3, pp. 187–209, 2010.

[NOY 12] NOYER J.-M., Les espaces immersifs: le plissement numérique du monde, anthropocène et immunopolitique, HAL - Toulon, April 2012.

[NOY 17] NOYER J.-M., "L'Internet des objets, l'Internet of "Everything" quelques remarques sur l'intensification du plissement numérique du monde", *Internet des objets*, vol. 1, no. 1, available at: https://www.openscience.fr/L-Internet-des-Objets-l-Internet-of-Everything-quelques-remarques-sur-l, 2017.

[PAG 17] PAGE C.L., Simulation multi-agent interactive: engager des populations locales dans la modélisation des socio-écosystèmes pour stimuler l'apprentissage social, HDR, 2017.

[PAR 16] PARISI L., "La raison instrumentale, le capitalisme algorithmique et l'incomputable", *Multitudes*, no. 62, pp. 98–109, 2016.

[PED 06] PEDAUQUE R.T., "Document et modernités", @SIC, 2006.

[PED 07] PEDAUQUE R.T., *La Redocumentarisation du monde*, Éditions Cépaduès, Toulouse, 2007.

[PER 16] PERCHY Y.S., Opinions, lies and knowledge. An algebraic approach to mobility of information and processes, PhD thesis, University Paris-Saclay, 2016.

[PLU 91] PLUTCHIK R., *The Emotions*, University Press of America, MD, 1991.

[POU 12] POUPYREV I., SCHOESSLER P., LOH J. *et al.*, "Botanicus interacticus: interactive plants technology", *ACM SIGGRAPH 2012 Emerging Technologies*, ACM, New York, pp. 1–4, 2012.

[PRE 16] PREVOT A.-C., DOZIERES A., TURPIN S. *et al.*, "Les réseaux volontaires d'observateurs de la biodiversité (Vigie-nature): quelles opportunités d'apprentissage?", *Cahiers de l'action*, no. 47, pp. 35–40, 2016.

[PRI 11] PRIE Y., Vers une phénoménologie des inscriptions numériques. Dynamique de l'activité et des structures informationnelles dans les systèmes d'interprétation, HDR, Claude Bernard University, Lyon I, 2011.

[QUE 13] QUEYROI F., Partitionnement de grands graphes: mesures, algorithmes et visualisation, PhD thesis, Agence bibliographique de l'enseignement supérieur, Montpellier, 2013.

[RAB 05] RABARDEL P., "Instrument subjectif et développement du pouvoir d'agir", *Modèles du sujet pour la conception: dialectiques, activités, développement*, Octarès Editions, Toulouse, 2005.

[RAB 10] RABOUIN D., *Vivre ici, Spinoza, éthique locale*, PUF, Paris, 2010.

[RAS 99] RASTIER F., "De la signification au sens. Pour une sémiotique sans ontologie", available at: http://www.revue-texto.net/index.php?id=560, 1999.

[RAS 08] RASTIER F., "Sémantique du web vs semantic web?", available at: http://www.revue-texto.net/index.php?id=1729, 2008.

[RAS 09] RASTIER F., *Sémantique interprétative*, PUF, Paris, 2009.

[REY 17] REYES-GARCIA E., BOUHAI N., *Designing Interactive Hypermedia Systems*, ISTE Ltd, London and John Wiley & Sons, New York, 2017.

[ROB 06] ROBIN J., GUATTARI F., "Révolution informatique, écologie et recomposition subjective", *Multitudes*, vol. 24, no. 1, pp. 131–143, 2006.

[ROQ 09] ROQUES P., *UML par la pratique*, Eyrolles, Paris, 2009.

[ROS 13] ROSENBERG D., GRAFTON A.T., GUILLON M.-C., *Cartographie du temps: des frises chronologiques aux nouvelles timelines*, Eyrolles, Paris, 2013.

[SAB 13] SABRI L., Modèles sémantiques, raisonnements réactif et narratif, pour la gestion du contexte en intelligence ambiante et en robotique ubiquitaire, PhD thesis, University Paris-Est, 2013.

[SAD 15] SADIN E., *La Vie algorithmique: critique de la raison numérique*, L'échappée, Paris, 2015.

[SAL 92] SALEH I., *Les Bases de données avancées*, Hermès, Paris, 1992.

[SAL 99] SALEH I., PAPY F., *Les Bases de données pour l'Internet et l'intranet*, Hermès, Paris, 1999.

[SAL 17] SALEH I., "Les enjeux et les défis de l'Internet des Objets (IdO)", *Internet des objets*, vol. 1, no. 1, 2017.

[SAN 00] SANDER E., *L'Analogie, du naïf au créatif: analogie et catégorisation*, L'Harmattan, Paris, 2000.

[SAN 08] SANDER E., "Les connaissances naïves en mathématiques", *Les Connaissances naïves*, Armand Colin, Paris, 2008.

[SER 90] SERRES M., *Le Système de Leibniz et ses modèles mathématiques*, PUF, Paris, 1990.

[SER 97] SERRES M., *Atlas*, Flammarion, Paris, 1997.

[SER 09] SERRES M., *Écrivains, savants et philosophes font le tour du monde*, Pommier, Paris, 2009.

[SER 10] SERRES A., DUPLESSIS P., LE DEUFF O. *et al.*, "Culture informationnelle et didactique de l'information. Synthèse des travaux du GRCDI, 2007-2010", *@SIC*, 2010.

[SLO 02] SLOTERDIJK P., *Sphères, microsphérologie. Tome 1, Bulles*, Pauvert, Paris, 2002.

[SLO 06] SLOTERDIJK P., *Sphères. Tome 3, Ecumes, Sphérologie plurielle*, Hachette Littératures, 2006.

[SLO 11] SLOTERDIJK P., *Globes: Sphères II*, Fayard/Pluriel, Paris, 2011.

[SON 13] SONNAC N., "L'écosystème des médias", *Communication. Information médias théories pratiques*, vol. 32, no. 2, available at: https://communication.revues.org/5030, 2013.

[STE 10] STEELE J., ILIINSKY N., *Beautiful Visualization*, O'Reilly Media, 2010.

[STI 04] STIEGLER B., *De la misère symbolique: tome 1. L'époque hyperindustrielle*, Galilée, Paris, 2004.

[STI 05] STIEGLER B., *De la misère symbolique: tome 2, La catastrophe du sensible*, Galilée, Paris, 2005.

[STI 06] STIEGLER B., "De l'économie libidinale à l'écologie de l'esprit", *Multitudes*, vol. 24, no. 1, pp. 85–95, 2006.

[SZO 10] SZONIECKY S., "Agent ontologique pour la veille des écosystèmes d'information", *Veille stratégique scientifique & technologique systèmes d'information élaborée, Bibliométrie*, Toulouse, France, 2010.

[SZO 11a] SZONIECKY S., "Proposition d'une méthode graphique pour le filtrage des flux d'information", *Doctorales SFIC 2011, Problématisation et méthodologie de recherche*, Bordeaux, France, 2011.

[SZO 11b] SZONIECKY S., "Le langage du Web du symbolique à l'allégorique, vers une représentation de la connaissance en train de se faire", *ISKO – Maghreb 2011*, Hammamet, Tunisia, 2011.

[SZO 12a] SZONIECKY S., "Les frontières des écosystèmes d'informations numériques", *Géoartistique et géopolitique frontières*, pp. 65–76, L'Harmattan, Paris, 2012.

[SZO 12b] SZONIECKY S., YACOUB C., "Les petites bibliothèques dans l'écosystème d'information mondiale", *Métiers de l'information, des bibliothèques et des archives*, pp. 131–144, Tunis, Tunisia, 2012.

[SZO 12c] SZONIECKY S., Évaluation et conception d'un langage symbolique pour l'intelligence collective : vers un langage allégorique pour le Web, Information and Communication Science, PhD thesis, University Paris VIII, Vincennes-Saint Denis, 2012.

[SZO 12d] SZONIECKY S., "Tweet Palette: cartographie sémantique pour l'interprétation d'un événement", *EUTIC 2012 Enjeux et usages des TIC: Publics et pratiques médiatiques*, p. 15, University of Lorraine, 2012.

[SZO 14a] SZONIECKY S., HACHOUR H., "Monades pour une éthique des écosystèmes d'information numériques", *Digital Intelligence*, Nantes, France, 2014.

[SZO 14b] SZONIECKY S., "Écosystème d'information pour la création, l'édition et l'évaluation de ressources pédagogiques numériques", *ICHSL9: Alternative Learning Systems*, Cotonou, Benin, 2014.

[SZO 15] SZONIECKY S., "Interpréter la voix de Deleuze. Exemple de jardinage des connaissances", in *Frontières d'archives Recherches, mémoires, savoirs*, pp. 165–177, Éditions des archives contemporaines, Paris, 2015.

[SZO 17a] SZONIECKY S., SAFIN S., "Modélisation éthique de l'Internet des objets", *Internet des objets*, vol. 2, no. 2, available at: https://www.openscience.fr/Modelisation-ethique-de-l-Internet-des-Objets, 2017.

[SZO 17b] SZONIECKY S., BOUHAÏ N., *Collective Intelligence and Digital Archives*, ISTE Ltd, London and John Wiley & Sons, New York, 2017.

[TER 15] TER BRAAKE S., FOKKENS A.S., "How to Make it in History. Working towards a Methodology of Canon Research with Digital Methods", *Proceedings of the First Conference on Biographical Data in a Digital World (BD2015)*, Amsterdam, 2015.

[THI 06] THIEVRE J., Cartographies pour la recherche et l'exploration de données documentaires, Informatique, PhD thesis, University of Montpellier II, France, 2006.

[TRI 06] TRICOT C., Cartographie sémantique des connaissances à la carte, PhD thesis, Computer science, University Savoie-Mont-Blanc, France, 2006.

[VAR 10] VARZI A.C., *Ontologie*, Éditions d'Ithaque, Paris, 2010.

[VIE 15] VIEIRA L., "Les écosystèmes numériques: le Big Bang. Aux sources des logiques de l'information en réseau", *Les écosystèmes numériques et la démocratisation informationnelle: Intelligence collective, Développement durable, Interculturalité, Transfert de connaissances*, Fort-de-France, France, 2015.

[WAN 05] WANDJI E.V., Analyse et formalisation ontologique des procédures de mesures associées aux méthodes de mesure de la taille fonctionnelle des logiciels: de nouvelles perspectives pour la mesure, Informatique cognitive, University of Québec, PhD thesis, Montreal, 2005.

[WIE 06] WIERZBICKA A., "Sens et grammaire universelle: théorie et constats empiriques", *Linx. Revue des linguistes de l'Université Paris X Nanterre*, no. 54, pp. 181–207, 2006.

[ZAC 10a] ZACKLAD M., "Introduction aux appareils de capture sémantique dans les TIC et les SI", in JUANALS B., NOYER J.-M. (eds), *Technologies de l'information et intelligences collectives*, Hermès-Lavoisier, Paris, 2010.

[ZAC 10b] ZACKLAD M., "Évaluation des systèmes d'organisation des connaissances", *Les Cahiers du numérique*, vol. 6, no. 3, pp. 133–166, 2010.

[ZAM 03] ZAMORA J.M., "La chôra après Platon", *Symboliques et dynamiques de l'espace*, pp. 16–32, Publication Université de Rouen-Havre, Mont Saint-Aignan, 2003.

Index

Other titles from

in

Information Systems, Web and Pervasive Computing

2018

ARDUIN Pierre-Emmanuel
Insider Threats
(Advances in Information Systems Set – Volume 10)

CHAMOUX Jean-Pierre
The Digital Era 1: Big Data Stakes

FABRE Renaud, BENSOUSSAN Alain
The Digital Factory for Knowledge: Production and Validation of Scientific Results

GAUDIN Thierry, LACROIX Dominique, MAUREL Marie-Christine, POMEROL Jean-Charles
Life Sciences, Information Sciences

GAYARD Laurent
Darknet: Geopolitics and Uses
(Computing and Connected Society Set – Volume 2)

IAFRATE Fernando
Artificial Intelligence and Big Data: The Birth of a New Intelligence
(Advances in Information Systems Set – Volume 8)

LE DEUFF Olivier
Digital Humanities: History and Development
(Intellectual Technologies Set – Volume 4)

MANDRAN Nadine
Traceable Human Experiment Design Research: Theoretical Model and
Practical Guide
(Advances in Information Systems Set – Volume 9)

2017

BOUHAÏ Nasreddine, SALEH Imad
Internet of Things: Evolutions and Innovations
(Digital Tools and Uses Set – Volume 4)

DUONG Véronique
Baidu SEO: Challenges and Intricacies of Marketing in China

LESAS Anne-Marie, MIRANDA Serge
The Art and Science of NFC Programming
(Intellectual Technologies Set – Volume 3)

LIEM André
Prospective Ergonomics
(Human-Machine Interaction Set – Volume 4)

MARSAULT Xavier
Eco-generative Design for Early Stages of Architecture
(Architecture and Computer Science Set – Volume 1)

REYES-GARCIA Everardo
The Image-Interface: Graphical Supports for Visual Information
(Digital Tools and Uses Set – Volume 3)

REYES-GARCIA Everardo, BOUHAÏ Nasreddine
Designing Interactive Hypermedia Systems
(Digital Tools and Uses Set – Volume 2)

SAÏD Karim, BAHRI KORBI Fadia
Asymmetric Alliances and Information Systems: Issues and Prospects
(Advances in Information Systems Set – Volume 7)

SZONIECKY Samuel, BOUHAÏ Nasreddine
Collective Intelligence and Digital Archives: Towards Knowledge Ecosystems
(Digital Tools and Uses Set – Volume 1)

2016

BEN CHOUIKHA Mona
Organizational Design for Knowledge Management

BERTOLO David
Interactions on Digital Tablets in the Context of 3D Geometry Learning
(Human-Machine Interaction Set – Volume 2)

BOUVARD Patricia, SUZANNE Hervé
Collective Intelligence Development in Business

EL FALLAH SEGHROUCHNI Amal, ISHIKAWA Fuyuki, HÉRAULT Laurent, TOKUDA Hideyuki
Enablers for Smart Cities

FABRE Renaud, in collaboration with MESSERSCHMIDT-MARIET Quentin, HOLVOET Margot
New Challenges for Knowledge

GAUDIELLO Ilaria, ZIBETTI Elisabetta
Learning Robotics, with Robotics, by Robotics
(Human-Machine Interaction Set – Volume 3)

HENROTIN Joseph
The Art of War in the Network Age
(Intellectual Technologies Set – Volume 1)

KITAJIMA Munéo
Memory and Action Selection in Human–Machine Interaction
(Human–Machine Interaction Set – Volume 1)

LAGRAÑA Fernando
E-mail and Behavioral Changes: Uses and Misuses of Electronic Communications

LEIGNEL Jean-Louis, UNGARO Thierry, STAAR Adrien
Digital Transformation
(Advances in Information Systems Set – Volume 6)

NOYER Jean-Max
Transformation of Collective Intelligences
(Intellectual Technologies Set – Volume 2)

VENTRE Daniel
Information Warfare – 2nd edition

VITALIS André
The Uncertain Digital Revolution
(Computing and Connected Society Set – Volume 1)

2015

ARDUIN Pierre-Emmanuel, GRUNDSTEIN Michel, ROSENTHAL-SABROUX Camille
Information and Knowledge System
(Advances in Information Systems Set – Volume 2)

BÉRANGER Jérôme
Medical Information Systems Ethics

BRONNER Gérald
Belief and Misbelief Asymmetry on the Internet

IAFRATE Fernando
From Big Data to Smart Data
(Advances in Information Systems Set – Volume 1)

KRICHEN Saoussen, BEN JOUIDA Sihem
Supply Chain Management and its Applications in Computer Science

NEGRE Elsa
Information and Recommender Systems
(Advances in Information Systems Set – Volume 4)

POMEROL Jean-Charles, EPELBOIN Yves, THOURY Claire
MOOCs

SALLES Maryse
Decision-Making and the Information System
(Advances in Information Systems Set – Volume 3)

SAMARA Tarek
ERP and Information Systems: Integration or Disintegration
(Advances in Information Systems Set – Volume 5)

2014

DINET Jérôme
Information Retrieval in Digital Environments

HÉNO Raphaële, CHANDELIER Laure
3D Modeling of Buildings: Outstanding Sites

KEMBELLEC Gérald, CHARTRON Ghislaine, SALEH Imad
Recommender Systems

MATHIAN Hélène, SANDERS Lena
Spatio-temporal Approaches: Geographic Objects and Change Process

PLANTIN Jean-Christophe
Participatory Mapping

VENTRE Daniel
Chinese Cybersecurity and Defense

2013

BERNIK Igor
Cybercrime and Cyberwarfare

CAPET Philippe, DELAVALLADE Thomas
Information Evaluation

LEBRATY Jean-Fabrice, LOBRE-LEBRATY Katia
Crowdsourcing: One Step Beyond

SALLABERRY Christian
Geographical Information Retrieval in Textual Corpora

CARREGA Pierre
Geographical Information and Climatology

CAUVIN Colette, ESCOBAR Francisco, SERRADJ Aziz
Thematic Cartography – 3-volume series
Thematic Cartography and Transformations – Volume 1
Cartography and the Impact of the Quantitative Revolution – Volume 2
New Approaches in Thematic Cartography – Volume 3

LANGLOIS Patrice
Simulation of Complex Systems in GIS

MATHIS Philippe
Graphs and Networks – 2ⁿᵈ edition

THERIAULT Marius, DES ROSIERS François
Modeling Urban Dynamics

2009

BONNET Pierre, DETAVERNIER Jean-Michel, VAUQUIER Dominique
Sustainable IT Architecture: the Progressive Way of Overhauling Information Systems with SOA

PAPY Fabrice
Information Science

RIVARD François, ABOU HARB Georges, MERET Philippe
The Transverse Information System

ROCHE Stéphane, CARON Claude
Organizational Facets of GIS

2008

BRUGNOT Gérard
Spatial Management of Risks

FINKE Gerd
Operations Research and Networks

GUERMOND Yves
Modeling Process in Geography

KANEVSKI Michael
Advanced Mapping of Environmental Data

MANOUVRIER Bernard, LAURENT Ménard
Application Integration: EAI, B2B, BPM and SOA

PAPY Fabrice
Digital Libraries

2007

DOBESCH Hartwig, DUMOLARD Pierre, DYRAS Izabela
Spatial Interpolation for Climate Data

SANDERS Lena
Models in Spatial Analysis

2006

CLIQUET Gérard
Geomarketing

CORNIOU Jean-Pierre
Looking Back and Going Forward in IT

DEVILLERS Rodolphe, JEANSOULIN Robert
Fundamentals of Spatial Data Quality

Printed and bound by CPI Group (UK) Ltd, Croydon, CR0 4YY